The World Trade Center Attack

Other books in the History Firsthand series:

The Civil War: The North
The Civil War: The South
The Constitutional Convention
The Gold Rush
The Great Depression
The Holocaust: Death Camps
Japanese American Internment Camps
Making and Using the Atomic Bomb
The Middle Ages
The Nuremberg Trial
Pioneers
Prohibition
The Renaissance
The Roaring Twenties
Sixties Counterculture
Slavery
The Vietnam War
War-Torn Bosnia
Women's Suffrage

The World Trade Center Attack

Tamara L. Roleff, *Book Editor*

Daniel Leone, *President*
Bonnie Szumski, *Publisher*
Scott Barbour, *Managing Editor*
David M. Haugen, *Series Editor*

GREENHAVEN
PRESS ®

THOMSON
<hr>
GALE

San Diego • Detroit • New York • San Francisco • Cleveland
New Haven, Conn. • Waterville, Maine • London • Munich

Cover credit: © Andrea Booher/FEMA News Photo
FEMA, 22
Photodisc, 18

LIBRARY OF CONGRESS CATALOGING-IN-PUBLICATION DATA

The World Trade Center attack / Tamara L. Roleff, book editor.
   p. cm. — (History firsthand)
Includes bibliographical references and index.
ISBN 0-7377-1469-7 (pbk. : alk. paper) — ISBN 0-7377-1468-9 (lib. : alk. paper)
   1. September 11 Terrorist Attacks, 2001—Personal narratives. 2. World Trade Center (New York, N.Y.) 3. Terrorism—New York (State)—New York. 4. Rescue work—New York (State)—New York. 5. September 11 Terrorist Attacks, 2001—Foreign public opinion. I. Roleff, Tamara L., 1959– . II. Series.
HV6432.7 .W67 2003
974.7'1044—dc21
                        2002029813

Printed in the United States of America

Contents

Foreword   11

Introduction: The Tragedy of September 11   13

Chapter 1: The Towers Collapse

Chapter Preface   31

1. Inside Tower One
by John Labriola   33
A man was in a meeting on the seventy-first floor of
the World Trade Center Tower One when the building
was hit by a hijacked airplane. People evacuated the
building in an orderly manner. About halfway down
the stairs, the evacuees met firefighters who were on
their way up to battle the fires. Shortly after the man
reached the street, the first tower collapsed.

2. Escape from Above the Impact Zone in Tower Two
by Brian Clark   38
An executive vice president of a brokerage firm on the
eighty-fourth floor of Tower Two was one of only four
people from above the impact zone who escaped from
the building. On his way down the stairs, he freed a
man who was trapped by debris, and the two men
barely made it out of the tower before it collapsed.

3. Trapped in the North Tower
by Dave Lim   51
A Port Authority police officer was in Tower Two
when he heard the plane hit Tower One. He left his
bomb-detection dog in his office and ran to the other
building to help. He was in the stairway when the
building collapsed and was trapped there for several
hours. When he was freed, he tried to return to his office to get his dog, but the animal was buried under
tons of rubble.

4. People Are Jumping
by Conor O'Clery   56
A newspaper reporter working in a building near the
World Trade Center witnessed the second plane fly

into the south tower. He saw people hang out of the building's windows and fall or jump one hundred stories to their deaths. Shortly after, he watched the collapse of both towers.

5. **Watching the Towers Fall**
   by Timothy Townsend   61
   A spectator watched the twin towers burn from the street. When the first tower collapsed, he ran for his life, trying to escape the huge cloud of dust and debris. Shortly after, the second tower fell. Eventually, he made it home and realized a friend was not so lucky.

6. **A Burn Victim at the World Trade Center**
   by Greg Manning   67
   A woman was severely burned by an explosive fireball as she entered the lobby of the World Trade Center. Bystanders helped put out the flames and she was rushed to a hospital. Her husband described the first few days of her recovery.

Chapter 2: Rescue and Recovery

Chapter Preface   75

1. **Saving Josephine**
   by Jay Jonas   77
   When the south tower collapsed, a unit of firefighters in the north tower decided to evacuate. Along the way, the firefighters found a woman who needed help getting down the stairs. When they got to the fourth floor, the north tower collapsed, but miraculously, the unit and the woman were still alive. Hours later, the group was rescued.

2. **A Firefighter's Worst Nightmare**
   by Dennis Smith   92
   Hearing news of the tragedy, a retired firefighter joined his old unit and went to the World Trade Center to help the rescue effort. The destruction and devastation at Ground Zero were beyond any firefighter's worst nightmare. Many of his friends and former colleagues were killed both before and after the buildings collapsed.

3. **Counting Bodies**
   by Sandeep Jauhar   97
   A doctor who went to Ground Zero to help ended up
   working at the makeshift morgue. Bodies—or, rather,
   pieces of bodies—were brought to the morgue, where
   they were cataloged and put aside. The doctor felt
   helpless in the face of such grim work.

4. **Searching for Bodies**
   by Paul Morgan   100
   A rescuer and his search dog entered Ground Zero
   looking for bodies buried under the pile of rubble.
   The work was difficult, but rewarding in a way; his
   dog found three bodies in thirty minutes. The handler
   and his dog left the site exhausted and in pain, but
   were overwhelmed by the kindness of others.

5. **A Priest at Ground Zero**
   by James Martin   104
   A priest visited a trauma center near the World Trade
   Center but discovered his help was not needed there.
   He then volunteered to go to Ground Zero, and his
   offer was eagerly accepted. There, he talked to firefighters, police officers, and rescuers, and was awed
   and inspired by their willingness to lay down their
   lives for others.

6. **A Night at Ground Zero**
   by Erin Bertocci   110
   A New Yorker wishing she could do more to help the
   rescue effort heard that the rescuers wanted coffee.
   She and her roommate collected coffee, pizza, and
   water and ventured down to the World Trade Center.
   She spent the night reorganizing the donated supplies,
   insisting it was a privilege to help out.

Chapter 3: The Western World's Response
Chapter Preface   116

1. **America Will Withstand This Attack**
   by George W. Bush   118
   The American president gave a televised speech to
   console the public after the attacks. He assured them
   that the country was strong and would recover. In ad-

dition, he said that the full resources of the government were being devoted to searching for those responsible and bringing them to justice.

2. **The World Must Unite Against Terrorists**
   by Tony Blair   121
   In a speech to the House of Commons, Great
   Britain's prime minister asserted that the terrorists
   behind the September 11 attacks against the United
   States were a threat not just to America but to the entire world. He urged all civilized countries to unite in
   an effort to eradicate terrorism.

3. **Americans Are Strong and Resilient**
   by Rudy Giuliani   127
   The mayor of New York City offered a prayer for
   America twelve days after the terrorist attack. He
   proclaimed that all the victims of September 11 were
   heroes and innocent of the tragedy that befell them.
   He asserted that the American people are resilient and
   assured them that they would emerge from this catastrophe stronger than ever.

4. **"We Stand by You"**
   by Megan Hallinan   131
   A navy officer sent an e-mail to her father describing
   an encounter at sea with a German ship that displayed
   a message of friendship and sympathy. The demon-
   stration of international solidarity was inspiring to all
   who witnessed it.

5. **Renewed Patriotism**
   by Michele Wallace Campanelli   133
   After the attacks of September 11, a woman tried to
   buy an American flag to fly outside her home as a
   symbol of patriotism. She was unable to find a flag
   despite visiting many stores and online businesses.
   Finally, her grandfather gave her a small flag, which
   she proudly flew alongside the many already flying in
   her community.

6. **Neighborly Concern**
   by Elizabeth Grove   137
   As the days passed after September 11, people real-
   ized what was important in life and became more po-

lite toward each other. New Yorkers watched to see if their neighbors came home after the attacks and they felt a profound sense of relief when a neighbor's light turned on and signaled all was well.

7. **Racist Assumptions**
   by Bob Levey   142
   A man—a well-dressed American businessman of
   Arab descent—was accused by an American woman
   of being sympathetic to the September 11 terrorists
   because of his ethnicity. In order to successfully battle terrorism, people must not judge others based on
   their race or heritage.

Chapter 4: The Arab World's Response

Chapter Preface   147

1. **"Hypocrisy Rears Its Ugly Head"**
   by Osama bin Laden   149
   The United States deserved the attacks against it, proclaimed the head of the al-Qaeda terrorist network in
   a prerecorded videotape. According to the message,
   America was hypocritical because it killed thousands
   of Muslims every day through its policies in the
   Middle East and yet it protested when its victims rose
   up against it.

2. **No Tears for America**
   by Muhammad Abbas   152
   A Muslim claimed he could not cry for Americans because he had no more tears left. All his tears had been
   for Palestinian martyrs who had given their lives trying to save their homeland from Americans and Jews.

3. **Americans Are Terrorists**
   by Sulaiman Abu Ghaith   154
   A spokesman for the al-Qaeda network asserts that
   Americans and Zionists are the true terrorists—they
   have been trying to rid the Middle East of Palestinians
   for decades. It is not terrorism when Muslims rise up
   against their oppressors. This is a battle between the
   faithful Muslims and the faithless infidel Americans.

4. A Vision of Plane Crashes
by Osama bin Laden   157
In a meeting with supporters, Osama bin Laden
claims to have known about the attacks against the
United States days before they occurred. His followers tell him that Islam remains strong and has gained
many new converts since the attacks.

5. Islamic Law Prohibits Harming the Innocent
by Salih bin Muhammad Al-Luheidan   166
An Islamic judge in Saudi Arabia asserts that Islam
does not condone harming or killing innocent people,
even in times of war. Those who claim that Islam
supports such actions are totally wrong.

Appendix: The Evidence Against Osama bin Laden
    and al-Qaeda   171
Chronology   187
For Further Research   193
Index   196

Foreword

In his preface to a book on the events leading to the Civil War, Stephen B. Oates, the historian and biographer of Abraham Lincoln, John Brown, and other noteworthy American historical figures, explained the difficulty of writing history in the traditional third-person voice of the biographer and historian. "The trouble, I realized, was the detached third-person voice," wrote Oates. "It seemed to wring all the life out of my characters and the antebellum era." Indeed, how can a historian, even one as prominent as Oates, compete with the eloquent voices of Daniel Webster, Abraham Lincoln, Harriet Beecher Stowe, Frederick Douglass, and Robert E. Lee?

Oates's comment notwithstanding, every student of history, professional and amateur alike, can name a score of excellent accounts written in the traditional third-person voice of the historian that bring to life an event or an era and the people who lived through it. In *Battle Cry of Freedom*, James M. McPherson vividly re-creates the American Civil War. Barbara Tuchman's *The Guns of August* captures in sharp detail the tensions in Europe that led to the outbreak of World War I. Taylor Branch's *Parting the Waters* provides a detailed and dramatic account of the American Civil Rights Movement. The study of history would be impossible without such guiding texts.

Nonetheless, Oates's comment makes a compelling point. Often the most convincing tellers of history are those who lived through the event, the eyewitnesses who recorded their firsthand experiences in autobiographies, speeches, memoirs, journals, and letters. The Greenhaven Press History Firsthand series presents history through the words of first-person narrators. Each text in this series captures a significant historical era or event—the American Civil War, the

Great Depression, the Holocaust, the Roaring Twenties, the 1960s, the Vietnam War. Readers will investigate these historical eras and events by examining primary-source documents, authored by chroniclers both famous and little known. The texts in the History Firsthand series comprise the celebrated and familiar words of the presidents, generals, and famous men and women of letters who recorded their impressions for posterity, as well as the statements of the ordinary people who struggled to understand the storm of events around them—the foot soldiers who fought the great battles and their loved ones back home, the men and women who waited on the breadlines, the college students who marched in protest.

The texts in this series are particularly suited to students beginning serious historical study. By examining these firsthand documents, novice historians can begin to form their own insights and conclusions about the historical era or event under investigation. To aid the student in that process, the texts in the History Firsthand series include introductions that provide an overview of the era or event, timelines, and bibliographies that point the serious student toward key historical works for further study.

The study of history commences with an examination of words—the testimony of witnesses who lived through an era or event and left for future generations the task of making sense of their accounts. The Greenhaven Press History Firsthand series invites the beginner historian to commence the process of historical investigation by focusing on the words of those individuals who made history by living through it and recording their experiences firsthand.

Introduction: The Tragedy of September 11

September 11, 2001, was a warm and sunny morning with beautiful blue skies. It started out just like any other day—until just before 9:00 A.M. when the first of two hijacked airplanes crashed into the World Trade Center in New York City. At that moment, the innocence and security of a nation vanished as it was attacked by a little-understood enemy.

Motivation for the Attacks

Speculation about who was behind these hijackings—and two others that occurred in Washington, D.C., and Pennsylvania—settled quickly on Osama bin Laden and his supporters in the Arab world. Bin Laden is a wealthy Saudi businessman who started paramilitary camps in Afghanistan in the early 1980s to train Islamic extremists in combat skills and terrorism techniques. His organization was formed to fight the Russians who were then in Afghanistan. After the Red Army pulled out of Afghanistan in 1989 (following a decade of war), bin Laden and his network of supporters and terrorists, known as al-Qaeda (the Base), needed a new enemy to fight. It was not long before they turned their attention to the United States.

The Persian Gulf War (1990–1991) can be seen as the catalyst for bin Laden and al-Qaeda's crusade against the United States and its policies in the Middle East. In August 1990, President Saddam Hussein of Iraq invaded the neighboring country of Kuwait. The United States, under the leadership of President George H.W. Bush, assembled an international coalition to oppose the invasion and force Hussein to withdraw from Kuwait. With permission from the Saudi government, the United States deployed tens of thousands of troops and stationed them at bases in Saudi Arabia during and after the war. Some Muslims, however, were not happy about the presence of U.S. troops in Saudi Arabia, which is home to several Islamic holy sites. Bin Laden was particularly angry about American soldiers being stationed in his homeland. He believed that Westerners in Saudi Arabia defiled Islam and that their presence would lead to the eradication of Arabic religion, language, culture, and way of life. Although bin Laden was not an Islamic cleric, he issued several fatwas (religious decrees) against the United States. His original fatwa urged his supporters to attack American military personnel wherever they were found in the Middle East and Africa.

A year after the end of the Gulf War, al-Qaeda extended the fatwa against U.S. forces by staging an attack against the United States in New York City. On February 26, 1993, an Islamic extremist, Ramzi Yousef, led by Sheik Omar Abdel-Rahman hid a one-thousand-pound bomb in a rented truck and detonated it in the garage of the World Trade Center. Six people were killed in the explosion and more than one thousand were injured. The terrorists—whose aim was to cause both towers to collapse and fall on each other—underestimated the amount of explosives needed to bring the towers down. Eventually, Abdel-Rahman and Yousef were arrested, charged, and convicted of trying to blow up the World Trade Center and were sentenced to life in prison.

A Holy War Against America

The violence against Americans, however, continued. In October 1993 in Mogadishu, Somalia, Somali fighters, trained by bin Laden and his al-Qaeda network, killed eighteen American soldiers who were trying to capture a Somali warlord and his top aides. Then on June 25, 1996, in Riyadh, Saudi Arabia, a car bomb exploded next to Khobar Towers, a military barracks for U.S. Air Force personnel still stationed in the Middle East. Nineteen Americans were killed and hundreds more were wounded in the attack. Two months later, bin Laden declared a jihad (holy war) against Americans. Because the Saudi government would not listen to his demands to force the Americans to leave Saudi Arabia, bin Laden claimed it was the duty of every Muslim to push "the American enemy out of the holy land. . . . The ultimate aim of pleasing Allah . . . is to fight the enemy, in every aspects [sic] and in a complete manner."[1] Bin Laden had no trouble finding recruits for his holy war. Muslim youths were eager to fight the infidels, he asserted, because of the rewards they would receive in heaven after their death. As bin Laden's declaration of war stated,

> These youths know that their rewards in fighting you, the USA, is double their rewards in fighting some one else not from the people of the book [the Koran]. They have no intention except to enter paradise by killing you.[2]

Bin Laden went on to exhort his followers: "It is a duty now on every tribe in the Arab Peninsula to fight, Jihad, in the cause of Allah and to cleanse the land from those occupiers."[3] He reinforced his decree by issuing a second fatwa against Americans in 1998, calling for attacks against Americans anywhere in the world:

> The ruling to kill the Americans and their allies—civilian and military—is an individual duty for every Muslim who can do it in any country in which it is possible to do it, in order to liberate the al-Aqsa Mosque and the holy mosque [Mecca] from their grip, and in order for their armies to move out of all the lands of Islam, defeated and unable to threaten any Muslim. This is in accordance with the words of Mighty Allah, "and to fight the pagans all together as they fight you all together," and "fight them until there is no more tumult or oppression, and there prevail justice and faith in Allah."[4]

In 1998, bin Laden's operatives struck again against Americans, this time in Africa. On August 20, car bombs exploded almost simultaneously outside the American embassies in Tanzania and Nigeria, killing 234 people and wounding more than 5,000. The United States retaliated against bin Laden by launching cruise missiles at his training camps in Afghanistan and at a suspected nerve-gas manufacturing plant in Sudan, which he supposedly funded. A follower of bin Laden, Mohamed Rashed Daoud Al-Owhali, was immediately arrested in Pakistan on charges connected with the bombings and extradited to the United States for trial. In November 1998, bin Laden and his military commander Muhammad Atef were indicted for murder in connection with the bombings in Tanzania and Nigeria. Shortly after, the FBI added bin Laden to its Ten Most Wanted list.

Undaunted, al-Qaeda continued its holy war against the United States. Ahmed Ressam, an Algerian with ties to the al-Qaeda network, planned to welcome the year 2000 by planting a bomb at Los Angeles International Airport. "If everything went right and the bomb went off in the Los Angeles Airport, it would have been a devastating attack,"[5] asserted Terrence McKenna, a journalist who pieced together Ressam's plot for a documentary for the Canadian Broadcasting Corporation. But Ressam never made it to Los Angeles; he was stopped at Port Angeles, Washington, on the U.S.-Canadian border by a U.S. Customs official who thought Ressam looked nervous. An inspection of his rental car found more than one hundred pounds of powerful explosives in the trunk. Ressam was sentenced to 130 years in prison.

Bin Laden's followers' next attempt against the Americans was in October 2000. The target this time was the USS *Cole*, a destroyer that was docked in Aden, Yemen, for refueling. While in port, suicide terrorists linked to al-Qaeda piloted their small boat alongside the ship and detonated a bomb, which blasted a huge hole in the ship's side. The explosion killed seventeen American sailors and wounded thirty-nine. Despite being seriously damaged, the *Cole* returned to the fleet after fourteen months of repairs.

Even before the USS *Cole* attack, bin Laden's operatives were in the middle of planning their most daring mission yet—hijacking American airplanes and flying them into buildings that symbolized American economic, military, and political power. It was only after the attacks of September

11, 2001, when U.S. authorities began their investigation that they realized bin Laden and al-Qaeda had been meticulously planning and training for the attacks for years.

The Day of the Attack

In the very early morning of September 11, Mohamed Atta and Abdulaziz Alomari boarded a small commuter plane in Portland, Maine, for a flight to Boston. Authorities are still unsure why Atta and Alomari drove from Boston to Portland the day before, only to fly back to Boston the morning of September 11, since it exposed them to more airline scrutiny and the possibility of arrest. Once the two men arrived in Boston, they boarded American Airlines Flight 11 for Los Angeles, which took off on time at 7:59 A.M. Within the next fifteen minutes, United Airlines Flight 175, United Airlines Flight 93, and American Airlines Flight 77—all making transcontinental flights with relatively few passengers on board—took off from Boston; Newark, New Jersey; and Washington, D.C., respectively.

The first clue that American Airlines Flight 11 was not going smoothly was at 8:28 A.M. when an air traffic controller in Nashua, New Hampshire, heard part of a conversation from the plane's cockpit and realized the jet was being hijacked. Shortly after, the plane turned south toward New York City.

The sequence of the attacks is now horrifyingly familiar. At 8:46 A.M. Eastern Daylight Time (some accounts say 8:48 A.M.), American Airlines Flight 11, with ninety-two passengers and crew on board, including five hijackers, crashed into the ninety-fourth through ninety-eighth floors of the north tower of the World Trade Center. Few people realized at the time that a commercial jet had crashed into the building; most people thought the thunder of the plane crashing into the building was perhaps a sonic boom or even freak lightning on an otherwise beautiful sunny morning. Those who heard that a plane had crashed into the tower assumed it was a small private plane that had tragically flown off course. When United Airlines Flight 175, with five of

Prior to the terrorist attacks of September 11, 2001, the twin towers of the World Trade Center dominated the New York City skyline.

Atta's and Alomari's confederates plus sixty other passengers and crew, crashed into the seventy-eighth through eighty-fourth floors of the south tower of the World Trade Center fifteen minutes later, the world understood that these were deliberate attacks against the United States by an unknown enemy. This realization was confirmed less than thirty minutes later when President Bush called the crashes "an apparent terrorist attack on our country."[6]

The first plane that crashed into the World Trade Center went in nearly level, the second plane, however, had begun to bank to the left when it crashed into the tower, thus slicing through more floors. Since the towers were designed with a minimum of interior support beams, there was little to stop or slow the planes as they ripped through the buildings. Witnesses saw huge fireballs explode out the sides of the buildings. As the orange ball of flames and black smoke rose in the sky, debris began to rain down on the streets and spectators below—sheets of paper, desks and office chairs, pieces of the plane, and also, horrifyingly, human remains.

Within minutes, rescue and fire crews had arrived at Tower One and began setting up their command posts to start evacuating the buildings and fighting the fires. Paramedic Louis Garcia immediately saw people who needed his help. In a *Time* article, he is quoted as saying, "There were people running over to us burnt from head to toe. Their hair was burned off. There were compound fractures, arms and legs sticking out of the skin. One guy had no hair left on his head."[7] Unfortunately, two of the six victims in his first ambulance run died on their way to the hospital.

Many people working in the towers had been working there when Abdel-Rahman and Yousef tried to blow up the World Trade Center in 1993, so they were familiar with evacuation procedures. They grabbed their friends, briefcases, and purses and started heading down the stairs to safety. Many passed firefighters carrying hoses, axes, oxygen tanks, ropes, and other heavy gear who were climbing the stairs to fight the fires and rescue those who were trapped on the floors above. However, since the stairways and elevators were in the center of the towers, the planes' paths through the building had cut off escape routes from the point of impact. Some people above the crash sites tried to escape by going to the roof, but the smoke was too thick and the heat from the fires was too intense to permit helicopters to rescue those trapped on the roof. For those who were trapped in their offices, many broke their windows and tried to attract attention to their plight by waving shirts and jackets. Some desperate souls even jumped to their deaths rather than face the prospect of being burned alive in their offices. Several firefighters and evacuees were killed by falling bodies and debris.

The Pentagon Is Attacked

As millions of people around the world watched the towers burn on live television, they were stunned by the report that another plane had crashed, this time into the Pentagon in Washington, D.C. American Airlines Flight 77, which had taken off at 8:10 A.M. from Washington's Dulles Airport en route to Los Angeles, crashed at 9:43 A.M. into the west side of the Pentagon. Witnesses said the pilot pushed the throttle to full speed as the plane flew low above the ground toward the building. Then a wing caught the ground and the plane cartwheeled into the Pentagon. Killed in the crash were 125 military and civilian employees at the Pentagon, 59 passengers and crew, and 5 hijackers. Robert J. Jenkins, a colonel and chaplain with the U.S. Army, was in a meeting at the Pentagon when the plane hit. He joined a search-and-rescue team to go back into the burning building to look for survivors. He soon realized that the search was hopeless:

> Though we could see through the smoke, the fumes were so strong that after about a hundred feet in we had to withdraw back out into the courtyard to wait. We exited coughing and moved toward better air.
>
> The longer we waited the more we realized the chances of getting anyone else out alive were diminishing. The fire was spreading. We had no news.[8]

The White House and U.S. Capitol, among many other buildings in Washington, D.C., were immediately evacuated. In New York City, the bridges and tunnels into Manhattan were closed, and the Empire State Building, the United Nations building, and the Metropolitan Museum of Art were evacuated. A few minutes later, at 9:49 A.M., all flights in the United States were grounded by the Federal Aviation Administration for the first time in history. The FAA also ordered that all international flights bound for the United States turn back or be diverted. But aviation officials soon realized that there was one plane that had not responded to the calls to land at the nearest airport. United Airlines Flight 93, with forty-five people on board, had taken off from Newark, New Jersey, at 8:01 A.M. bound for San Francisco. Just west of Akron, Ohio, the plane turned back toward Washington, D.C.

United Airlines Flight 93

Air traffic controllers tried to contact the pilots but received no response. Other people, however, were contacted by passengers on the plane. An emergency dispatcher southeast of Pittsburgh, Pennsylvania, received a phone call at 9:58 A.M.

from a passenger who said he had locked himself in the plane's restroom. The man frantically told the dispatcher that United Airlines Flight 93 was in trouble: "We are being hijacked! We are being hijacked!"[9] Passenger Tom Burnett called his wife, Deena, shortly before 10:00 A.M. and told her his flight had been hijacked. During the next ten or fifteen minutes, Burnett called his wife four times, pumping her for information about the other hijacked airplanes and what had happened to them. She believed that her husband realized before she did that the hijackers did not want a ransom but were intent on a suicide mission. Deena Burnett recounted his final call to her for *Dateline NBC*'s Maria Shriver:

> He said, "OK, there's a group of us and we're going to do something." I said, "No." And I said, "Please sit down and be still, be quiet, don't draw attention to yourself." And he said, "No." He said, "If they're going to drive this plane into the ground . . . we've got to do something."[10]

Tom Burnett then hung up and it is believed that he joined passengers Jeremy Glick, Todd Beamer, Lou Nacke, and Mark Bingham in rushing the hijackers. Shortly after Burnett's last phone call to his wife, at 10:06 A.M., United Airlines Flight 93 crashed in Somerset County, Pennsylvania, killing all forty-five people aboard.

The Towers Collapse

As the drama was unfolding over the skies of Pennsylvania, one of the symbols of New York City disappeared from its skyline. Tower Two, the second tower hit by the hijacked airplane, collapsed. Thousands of people—office workers, firefighters, delivery workers, visitors, and others—were still inside the building when the beams supporting the upper stories buckled due to the fires' intense heat and were no longer able to support the weight. The tower pancaked. As one story fell, the floor below it was unable to support the additional weight, causing it to collapse, and so on and so on, until nothing was left of the building but a roiling cloud of gray dust. Barton Gellman, a correspondent for the *Wash-*

ington Post, was in New York City and witnessed the tower's disintegration into smoke and rubble:

> Everything got all mixed up in an almighty blow to the senses: a huge, low, rumbling, almost subsonic wave that resonated inside our bodies and filled our ears and seemed to go on a long time. I have felt only one thing at all like it before, while standing on a carrier flight deck for the launch of an F-14.
>
> At the same time the smoky blaze of the tower became a boiling black cloud. And when the cloud began to clear a few seconds later, the tower was simply not there. GONE!! I wrote stupidly on an index card, underlining it three times. I could think of nothing else to write.[11]

Tower One, the first building that was attacked, fell about thirty minutes later. Engineers later theorized that it held up longer before collapsing because the plane crashed higher into the building and therefore the upper support beams did not carry as much weight. Shortly after the second tower fell, the damaged portion of the Pentagon collapsed, and at 5:20 P.M., World Trade Center Seven, a forty-seven-story building that had been damaged when the twin towers fell, collapsed.

A mountain of rubble surrounds the remaining section of the World Trade Center shortly after the September 11 terrorist attacks.

Initial estimates of the dead and missing were staggering; some fifty thousand people were believed to have worked in the two towers. New York City mayor Rudy Giuliani said that no matter how many people died, "it will be more than we can bear."[12] As the days passed, the estimated number of deaths consistently fell; early reports had between five and seven thousand people dead or missing. As officials weeded through duplicate reports of missing persons, the number of dead and missing fell and finally hovered around three thousand. A website dedicated to the victims of the attacks, www.september11victims.com, updated the total daily. More than a year after the attacks, it listed 2,934 as confirmed dead; 40 reported dead; and 26 reported missing, for a total of 3,000 victims of the tragedy.

The War on Terrorism Begins

President Bush was in Florida on the morning of September 11, talking to children in a scheduled visit to an elementary school. After he returned to Washington, D.C., that evening, he addressed the nation, reassuring them that the government was doing everything possible to determine who was behind the attacks and to bring them to justice. Then, after meeting with members of his National Security Council, Bush spoke the words that people had been thinking:

> The deliberate and deadly attacks which were carried out yesterday against our country were more than acts of terror. They were acts of war. This will require our country to unite in steadfast determination and resolve. Freedom and democracy are under attack.[13]

Bush vowed that the United States would find its enemy wherever it was hiding and that it would not give up the battle until it was victorious in the war on terrorism.

Bush was not alone in proclaiming the attacks an act of war against the United States. Many of the country's allies immediately expressed their support in the hunt for those responsible. Prime Minister Tony Blair told his countrymen that Great Britain stood "shoulder to shoulder"[14] with the United States. And for the first time in its history the North Atlantic

Treaty Organization invoked Article Five of its charter:

> The Parties agree that an armed attack against one or more of
> them in Europe or North America shall be considered an attack
> against them all and consequently they agree that, if such an
> armed attack occurs, each of them . . . will assist the Party or Par-
> ties so attacked by taking forthwith, individually and in concert
> with the other Parties, such action as it deems necessary, includ-
> ing the use of armed force, to restore and maintain the security of
> the North Atlantic area.[15]

The United Nations followed with its own resolution, condemning the attacks and calling them "a threat to international peace and security."[16]

Following the Trail

Early in the morning of September 12, officials identified
five Arab men as suspects in the crashes. The FBI had been
able to determine who the suspected hijackers were so
quickly because of phone calls from passengers and flight
attendants aboard the doomed airplanes. Several people had
used their cell phones to alert the authorities that the planes
had been hijacked and to inform them of the hijackers' seat
numbers. In addition, a tip from a man who had had a con-
frontation with another driver in the parking garage of
Boston's Logan Airport led authorities to one of the hijackers' cars. Inside the car they found flight-training manuals
written in Arabic and a ramp pass that allowed access to re-
stricted areas of the airport. By the end of the week, the FBI
had identified nineteen hijackers and a man whom authorities suspected was supposed to have been the twentieth hijacker on United Airlines Flight 93 (he had been arrested on
unrelated charges in August).

Within days of the attacks, the FBI knew much about the
hijackers' backgrounds. The hijackers had lived quietly in
the United States for at least a year prior to the attacks, some
of them even longer. Six of them had taken flight lessons in
the United States. In 1997, Waleed Alshehri, a hijacker on
American Airlines Flight 11, which crashed into the north

tower of the World Trade Center, graduated from Embry-Riddle Aeronautical University in Daytona Beach, Florida, with a degree in aeronautical science and a commercial pilot's license. Hani Hanjour received his commercial pilot's license in 1999 while living in San Diego, California, with two other men, Nawaf Alhazmi and Khalid Almihdhar. These three men were aboard American Airlines Flight 77, which flew into the Pentagon in Washington, D.C. In July 2000, two of the hijackers—Atta (on board Flight 11) and Marwan Al-Shehhi (believed to be the pilot of Flight 175, which crashed into the south tower of the World Trade Center)—began flight lessons at a school in Venice, Florida.

Several of the pilots had problems learning how to fly, however. It took Hanjour more than three months to earn a private pilot's license that most students receive in four to six weeks. Then, long before they had accumulated the flight hours an airline would demand of a future pilot, Atta and Al-Shehhi paid the expensive fees needed to train for six hours in a jet simulator. It was not enough time to learn how to fly a jet, but it did give them the sense of what flying a commercial airliner was like, which was all they needed to know in order to fly their planes into the towers of the World Trade Center.

Zacarias Moussaoui had a different problem. He had told his instructors at a flight school in Minnesota that he was not interested in learning how to take off or land a plane; he wanted only to learn to fly it in midair. His instructors reported his suspicious behavior to the FBI and he was arrested in August 2001 on immigration charges. After the attacks of September 11, France informed the United States that Moussaoui was a suspected Islamic terrorist, and he was subsequently held on charges alleging that he was planning to be one of the hijackers on the planes on September 11.

Missed Clues

In the aftermath of the attacks, government agencies realized that they had collected information about the September 11 attacks but, due to interagency rivalries and bureaucratic infighting, had failed to share the information. Thus, the importance of the clues went unrealized. The FBI learned in July 2001 that bin Laden's al-Qaeda organization was planning a massive attack against the United States, but there were few details. Also in July, an FBI agent in Phoenix suggested that the agency look into the possibility that Islamic terrorists were studying at U.S. flight schools to learn how to hijack American planes. In addition, the National Security Agency intercepted a phone call on September 10, 2001, in which the speaker said in Arabic "Tomorrow is zero hour."[17] Unfortunately, the message was not translated from Arabic until September 12. Despite the fact that President George W. Bush was warned by the CIA several times during the summer of 2001 that Islamic extremists could be planning an attack against Americans (either through hijackings; car, truck, or boat bombs; or possibly even bioterrorism) the United States was unprepared for the attacks of September 11, 2001.

Blaming bin Laden

According to President Bush and Great Britain's Prime Minister Blair, the hijackers' trail led straight to al-Qaeda and its leader, bin Laden. Bush soon named bin Laden as the chief suspect behind the attacks on the United States. When a reporter asked Bush if he wanted bin Laden dead, Bush answered, "When I was a kid I remember that they used to put out there in the Old West, a wanted poster. It said: 'Wanted, Dead or Alive.' All I want and America wants [is] him brought to justice. That's what we want."[18]

A few days later, Bush spoke to both houses of Congress on live television. He officially named bin Laden and his al-Qaeda network as those responsible for the attacks on September 11. He told Americans that al-Qaeda intended to impose its radical religious beliefs on the world and it proposed to accomplish its goals by killing Christians and Jews, two groups it viewed as its archenemies. Bush also explained that al-Qaeda had a mutually supportive relationship with the government of Afghanistan—the Taliban. He condemned the Taliban regime for the oppression of its people and its support of bin Laden, al-Qaeda, and terrorism. He then listed the following demands to the Taliban:

> Deliver to United States authorities all the leaders of al-Qaeda who hide in your land. Release all foreign nationals, including American citizens, you have unjustly imprisoned. Protect foreign journalists, diplomats and aid workers in your country. Close immediately and permanently every terrorist training camp in Afghanistan, and hand over every terrorist, and every person in their support structure, to appropriate authorities. Give the United States full access to terrorist training camps, so we can make sure they are no longer operating.
>
> These demands are not open to negotiation or discussion. The Taliban must act, and act immediately. They will hand over the terrorists, or they will share in their fate.[19]

Bush warned Americans and the world that, should the Taliban not accede to these demands, the United States would begin its war to fight terrorism wherever it was found. It would not be an easy or a clean war; most likely, he told them, it would take a long time to fight, the United States would suffer casualties, and it would not end with a decisive liberation of occupied territory.

Bush also announced the formation of a new cabinet-level position: the Office of Homeland Security, whose mission would be coordinating among the dozens of federal departments and agencies involved a strategy to protect the United States. He named Pennsylvania governor Tom Ridge as the first director of homeland security.

The Taliban did not respond to Bush's calls to hand over bin Laden, the extremists he was training, or his training camps. By early October 2001, American military forces and carrier battle groups with their accompanying troops and bomber and fighter planes were in position in the Middle East. Great Britain, Canada, and other American allies also sent or promised military support. Then, on October 7, 2001, when the U.S. and allied military forces were in place, Bush ordered them to attack:

On my orders, the United States military has begun strikes against al-Qaeda terrorist training camps and military installations of the Taliban regime in Afghanistan. These carefully targeted actions are designed to disrupt the use of Afghanistan as a terrorist base of operations, and to attack the military capability of the Taliban regime.[20]

The War on Terror had begun.

Notes

1. Osama bin Laden, "Declaration of War Against the Americans Occupying the Land of Two Holy Places," in Yonah Alexander and Michael S. Swetnam, *Usama bin Laden's al-Qaida: Profile of a Terrorist Network.* Ardsley, NY: Transnational, 2001, Appendix 1A, pp. 6–7.

2. bin Laden, "Declaration of War," p. 16.

3. bin Laden, "Declaration of War," p. 19.

4. World Islamic Front Statement, "Jihad Against Jews and Crusaders," February 23, 1998. www.fas.org.

5. Quoted in Bob McKeown, "A Terrorist's Tale," October 1, 2001. www.msnbc.com.

6. George W. Bush, "Remarks by the President After Two Planes Crash into the World Trade Center," September 11, 2001. www.whitehouse.gov.

7. Quoted in Nancy Gibbs, "If You Want to Humble an Empire," *Time,* September 14, 2001, p. 35.

8. Robert J. Jenkins, "Pentagon Attack 11 September 2001." www.hooah4health.com.

9. Quoted in Gibbs, "If You Want to Humble an Empire," p. 40.

10. Quoted in Maria Shriver, "A Likely Hero," *Dateline NBC,* September 23, 2001. www.msnbc.com.

11. Barton Gellman, "The Cloud Rolled Toward Us, and We Had to Run," *American Journalism Review,* October 2001, p. 23.

12. Quoted in Gibbs, "If You Want to Humble an Empire," p. 32.

13. George W. Bush, "Remarks by the President in Photo Opportunity with the National Security Team," September 12, 2001. www.whitehouse.gov.

14. Tony Blair, "U.S. Attack: Prime Minister's Statement," September 11, 2001. www.pm.gov.uk.

15. North Atlantic Treaty Organization, "The North Atlantic Treaty," April 4, 1949. www.nato.int.

16. United Nations Security Council, "Resolution 1368 (2001)," September 12, 2001. www.un.org.
17. Quoted in *Time,* July 1, 2002, p. 16.
18. George W. Bush, "Remarks by the President to Employees at the Pentagon," September 17, 2001. www.whitehouse.gov.
19. George W. Bush, "Address to a Joint Session of Congress and the American People," September 20, 2001. www.whitehouse.gov.
20. George W. Bush, "Presidential Address to the Nation," October 7, 2001. www.whitehouse.gov.

Chapter 1

The Towers Collapse

Chapter Preface

At 8:46 A.M. on a beautiful Tuesday morning, a Boeing 767 flew straight into the World Trade Center. Most people, when they heard the initial reports of a plane flying into Tower One, immediately assumed it was a small, private plane whose pilot made a tragic error. But when the second jet crashed into Tower Two about fifteen minutes later, everyone knew the crashes were no accident. The United States was under attack by an unknown enemy.

The first plane, American Airlines Flight 11, en route from Boston to Los Angeles, had ninety-two passengers on board, including five Arab men assumed to be the hijackers. It crashed into Tower One between the ninety-fourth and ninety-eighth floors. United Airlines Flight 175, the second plane, was also en route to Los Angeles from Boston; it had sixty-five passengers on board, including five hijackers. At 9:03 A.M., banking hard to the left, the plane flew into Tower Two between the seventy-eighth and eighty-fourth floors. Explosions from both crashes burst out of all four sides of the towers, spewing out aircraft parts, office furniture, smoke, and flames. Papers, ash, broken glass, and body parts began to rain down on spectators on the streets below.

Almost immediately after the first crash, firefighters and rescue personnel appeared on the scene, ready to begin the long climb up to the upper stories to fight the fires and help rescue the people who were trapped or injured by the explosions. Those who were inside and made it out described an orderly evacuation down the stairwells. Many people stopped to help those who were disabled reach the ground floor safely. Some evacuees met firefighters and rescue workers who were on their way up and offered encouragement to keep climbing to where the fires were. People inside the first tower were shocked to discover that, while they were walking down the stairs, a second plane had been flown into Tower Two. Some emerged from Tower One to find that Tower Two had disappeared from the skyline.

The evacuees were not out of danger once they had made their way out of the towers and reached the street. They were still in danger of being hit by falling debris. Some people who were trapped on floors above the crash site felt they had no choice but to jump to their deaths, to the horror of people watching below. Others who were trapped broke out their office windows and clung to the steel support beams outside until they lost their grip and fell. Their hurtling bodies killed several people on the streets below.

The streets surrounding the towers were chaotic. They were filled with wreckage and rubble, and many were slick with blood from jumpers and plane victims. Once the towers collapsed, the air was filled with a thick gray dust that reduced visibility to just a few feet. The streets near Ground Zero became almost impassable, and hundreds of vehicles—and people—were crushed or injured by the falling buildings.

Inside Tower One

John Labriola

> The first hijacked plane crashed into Tower One of the World
> Trade Center between the ninety-fourth and ninety-eighth
> floors at about 8:46 A.M. John Labriola, a computer consul-
> tant who had been working for about two weeks for the Port
> Authority, was in a meeting on the seventy-first floor of the
> north tower (WTC 1) at the time of the crash. In the following
> essay, he describes how the building shuddered with the
> impact. He and his coworkers realized immediately that the
> tower had been hit by a plane and they started walking down
> the stairs to evacuate. Despite the confusion, heat, and stress,
> the evacuation was orderly and calm. About midway down
> the stairs they started meeting firefighters who were on their
> way up to fight the fires. As the evacuees got closer to ground
> level, they encountered water flowing down the stairs from
> broken sprinkler pipes. Labriola made it safely outside the
> building where he saw for the first time the devastation of
> both towers. When the towers fell, he took sanctuary in a
> nearby church. When the dust and debris had settled, he
> began making his way home to his family.

I was there. It is so terrible, but I'm ok. Many people
weren't so lucky. I had started a new contract for the Port
Authority(PA) about two weeks ago. I drove in that day
down the east river drive and parked in a lot three blocks
south of WTC 2 (World Trade Center Tower 2). The PA had
given me a cubicle on the south side of the 71st floor of
WTC1 (the north building).

At 8:30 A.M. I was in a status meeting on 71-East. The building rocked first in one direction then shuttered back and forth and finally settled. None of us were hurt or knocked off our seats but getting up while the building was moving was difficult. The building felt like it had moved at least five or six feet in each direction.

From the conference room door I could see out the window. The sky was so blue, papers were flying everywhere. It looked like a ticker tape parade. We were on the east side of the building. We speculated from the start that we were hit by a plane. I ran around the floor to the south side of the building and grabbed my backpack and laptop.

Going Down the Stairs

Everyone was off the floor pretty quickly. The guy I report to and I headed out to the lobby. One of the stairwells smelled strongly of smoke. The other seemed ok and we joined a group of others already beginning the walk down. Everyone handled it so well, we all helped each other. We walked down two by two stopping every so often for some unknown reason. Some people were helped down from higher floors with terrible burns over their bodies.

Whenever necessary we would press ourselves into a single file to let people get by. It was pretty hot, people were slipping on the sweat of the people who had come before them. In some places the smoke was worse than others. Thank god the lights always stayed on. People covered their mouths and eyes with whatever they had available.

When fears bubbled up there was always reassuring words from the right person that calmed even the most frightened of us. I was told from someone who was on 81 that there was fire on his floor immediately after the first plane struck. When the second plane struck we felt it, but had no idea what it was.

It wasn't until someone began getting news on his pager that we knew that a plane had hit each of the towers and the Pentagon. People constantly were checking their cell phones to see if there was service. Many of us had service but no calls could get out. I remember joking that we should all buy stock in the first company whose service worked.

Around the 35th floor we started meeting a steady stream of firefighters walking up and had to press into single file again. None of them said a word as they went up and past us carrying unbelievable loads of equipment. They were already exhausted by the time we started seeing them. I can't stop thinking about the look in their eyes and how heroic they were.

I pray some of them made it out. A few floors lower, water was flowing creating a rapids down the stairs. This got worse as we got lower down. The stairwell led down to an outside door lined with emergency workers urging us to move to safety. The courtyard where this outdoor landing led us onto must have been blocked or too dangerous for us to cross because we were directed back into the second floor balcony and down two escalators into the Mall under Tower 1.

Outside

Water was falling everywhere; 8 to 10 inches in some places. Many of the stores had windows blown out. All along the way emergency workers urged us to keep moving. I went up another escalator in the northeast corner of the mall and out onto Church Street. I was outside. In all it took 50 minutes to get down. As I stepped into the light emergency workers were yelling "don't look up; keep moving." I crossed the street and looked up. It was unreal. I saw someone fall from Tower 1.

Many people where just watching the buildings burn from Church Street up to Broadway. People I knew were helping each other gather themselves. I stopped to help calm a co-worker. I shared my cell phone with people desperate to get word to our loved ones that we were OK. The phone didn't work. We talked about what to do next. I looked at the ground around us and there was a lot of blood. Some shrapnel caught my attention. I couldn't stop thinking that it must have been from a plane.

Shoes were everywhere, newspapers and blood. When I looked up, the people I was with were gone. I thought I would head south toward my car so I headed down Broadway. The doors to Trinity Church were open so I stepped into Trinity Church. A priest was leading a prayer service, I knelt to say a quick prayer, minutes later the first building fell. The stained glass windows that were filled with color and light turned inky black.

You could feel it as much as hear the building collapse. Debris hit the roof of the church. People dove under pews. I looked out the front door. I couldn't see three feet in front of me. I thought it must be impossible to breathe outside. We gathered everyone inside the church, and made plans to evacuate; we searched the church, found some water, food and made up wet towels for people inside and out should we need to leave the protection of the church. We waited for the air outside to be clear enough to see. Someone found a radio and positioned it on a pulpit. It grew lighter outside the church. A few minutes later my cell phone rang; it was my mother-in-law calling from Holland.

I asked her to call my wife and mom. Up till this time no one's cell phones worked. I tried but still couldn't call out. In looking around the church I found a phone that worked and was able to get a call out to my wife at her office in midtown. She was devastated. She knew I was in the building as did some of my close friends whom I had spoken with at 8:15. She told me that my brother-in-law was on his way to get her and take her to his apartment in the West Village. I promised to meet her there. Then the second building fell.

Blackness again, larger objects were hitting the roof of the church. We had relatively clean air inside but there was a lot of deliberation about whether it was safer to stay in the church or take our chances outside. 40 minutes or so later it was again clear enough to see across the street. We said our goodbyes to each other and in groups of two and three ventured out to find a way home.

Finding a Way Home

There were three of us in my group. Outside was a mess. Winds would whip through the streets causing temporary white-outs blacking out the sun. I remember thinking that they must have been caused by the draft from the fire. Emergency vehicles caused their own white-outs and you would have to hide your faces as they came by. The group I left with headed south, then east, then north. We passed others leaving the area and some firefighters heading in. At the Water Street entrance to the Brooklyn Bridge we said goodbye to one of our party and two of us continued north through Chinatown into Soho. All along the way people were gathered in disbelief.

Radios drew larger crowds. I remember someone talking on a cell phone telling his friend that no one above the 60th floor could have gotten out. I told him that that wasn't true, that I had walked down from 71. He called after me, "Thank you, sir, thank you." I just kept walking. I stopped at different places where I knew that I should have seen the towers.

I made my way to my sister's house where my wife fell into my arms. I can't imagine what she felt like not knowing. I can't imagine what it's like for thousands of others whose loved ones didn't get home. My heart breaks for them. I don't know quite how to feel. From talking to people in the stairwell at least I know that some people up to the 81st floor got out ok. I'm grateful for that. I hope everyone got far enough away before the first building fell. I'm incredibly lucky, and incredibly sad. I'm angry but I'm more interested in reaching out and helping anyone I can get through this. I know the world has changed, and so have I.

Escape from Above the Impact Zone in Tower Two

Brian Clark

The second hijacked plane crashed into the south tower (WTC 2), between the seventy-eighth and eighty-fourth floors. Brian Clark is an executive vice president at Euro Brokers, a brokerage firm located on the eighty-fourth floor of Tower Two. He is one of only four people who escaped from either tower who were on floors above where the planes crashed. In the following essay, Clark provides an eyewitness account of the crash into Tower Two and his attempt to get his coworkers to evacuate the building by going down the stairs. Some people felt they would be safer going up to the building's roof, where they hoped to be rescued by helicopters. Tragically, they perished when the building collapsed. On Clark's way down the stairs, he heard a man calling for help and he stopped to help him get out from under debris. Then together the two men continued walking down the stairs, where they saw no one going down nor met anyone coming up. Clark had been out of the building about five minutes when Tower Two collapsed. Although Clark made it out alive, he lost more than sixty friends and coworkers in the attacks.

Like any normal day I arrived at about 7:15 in the morning. That particular day was more or less flawless weather—beautiful day, blue sky. I don't remember the temperature, but we had an unseasonably warm fall, and I'm assuming that that day was equally pleasant.

I have been at Euro Brokers for over 29 years now. I started as a trainee broker in 1973, and for the last 14 or 15 years I've been in management. Most recently my title's been Executive Vice President. I've been one of several people who manage the company. One minor responsibility I had that turned out to be significant that day, however, was I was one of about eight or ten people that had volunteered to be a fire marshal.

The First Plane

As I said, I arrived about 7:15 and got my morning coffee. I went about my normal chores. I don't really recall any extraordinary events that morning until 8:46 and change, when, sitting with my back to the west wall—I had a private office, with my desk facing my door and my back to the window—I heard an enormous *thump.* I didn't feel any vibration, but there was a noticeable sound like a *boom* or *thump,* and the lights buzzed for a second. My eyes jerked up to look at my overhead lights.

There was suddenly this glare, and my attention was immediately caught. I spun my head around, and the entire airspace behind me was filled with flame. I didn't know what it was at the time, but it was the fuel from the first jet hitting the North Tower that had gone right through that tower and out over the airspace, south of Tower One, the North Tower. That same airspace was west of the South Tower, the tower I was in on the 84th floor.

My immediate thought was there had been an explosion one or two floors above our office. That's what I thought had happened in that first instant. Being one of the fire marshals, I was equipped with a whistle and flashlight in my office. I jumped up, grabbed them, put the whistle around my neck, and more or less yelled, "Get out! Everybody get out!" This all took me five seconds. When I looked behind me out the window, the flames were all gone, and thousands of papers were just fluttering in the air, the edges of which were all on fire. It was like flaming confetti. Very strange.

I should have realized but didn't realize at the time that the area that all this was happening in was so huge. But I still wasn't computing that in my mind; still it was two floors up in my mind. So I ran out of my office, just a yard or two into an area where some accountants sit, and other people in offices, and I said, "Come on, let's go, there has been an explosion," and I started to get people off the floor.

Breaking News

Now, we are a trading operation. Our customers are not individuals, but large financial trading institutions around the world, like a Barclay's Bank or the Royal Bank of Canada. So we have in our trading floor many television sets tuned to financial news information. Well, all of these stations cut away to their news departments, and there were these breaking news stories that an airplane had hit the World Trade Center. The story developed literally within minutes, and we understood fairly soon, I would say within three or four minutes, that an airliner had hit One World Trade Center. At least that's my recollection of the timeframe.

Well, we knew now that the damage had been done to Tower One, not our Tower, so we relaxed a little bit about evacuation. Nonetheless, many people in the first minute had bolted for the stairs and were on their way down. Good news in retrospect, but at the time it was like, Oh boy, I guess we don't have to leave. The TV sets were telling us, and now there were photographs of One World Trade Center and the smoke coming out of the upper floors, I think the 92nd floor and above. The fire marshals like myself were content to let people go or stay. Really, in a way, it didn't matter.

I called my wife and told her, "You know, you won't believe this but Tower One has been hit. We are fine where we are. Relax, turn on the TV, there is a developing story there, find out what's happening."

The Announcement

At about five minutes to nine there was an announcement by the Port Authority within our building. First the strobe lights flashed, as they did during their normal fire drills. The alarm system gave a little bit of a *whoop whoop,* you know, to alert you to an announcement about to be made. Then the very familiar voice, the one we heard all the time, came over the system and said, "Building Two is secure. There is no need to evacuate Building Two. If you are in the midst of evacuation, you may return to your office by using the re-entry doors on the re-entry floors and the elevators to return to your office. Repeat, Building Two is secure. . . ."

And they went through the whole story again. So this was reinforcement that there was no need to evacuate. I am strictly guessing but I would think we were perhaps down to about 25 people left on our floor at the time of the announcement. (I had gone for a walk through our office.) Now, as I say, the pressure was off, and there wasn't a panic, although we were greatly concerned about what was going on in Tower One.

If you went to the north wall windows, you could look up and see the flames and the smoke and regrettably people now starting to jump, because of heat, smoke, or whatever it was. I'm only telling this secondhand because I personally could not take myself to the window to view that. I just didn't want that image burned in my brain, and I'm forever grateful that I didn't go and take in that sight.

One girl in particular—Susan her name was—turned from the window when she noticed the first person jump. She hadn't noticed it before, and she spun around in tears almost frantically, ran to me, and said "Oh, Brian, it's terrible. People are dying." I said, "Susan, it's a terrible tragedy," and I put my arms around her, and I said "Come on, let's get you more composed," and we walked out of the trading floor down the hall. In the building the center core was crossed hallways. There was a north-south hallway and an east-west hallway. I walked with her from the east side through the center core to the west side, where the ladies room was, and she went into the ladies room. (Regrettably, Susan did not survive the eventual collapse of the building.)

The Second Plane

I continued on to the west side near my office. I was fairly near the windows talking with two or three people, including Bobby Coll. I was looking him in the eye having a conversation with him when at apparently 9:03—I didn't check my watch—the second plane hit the south side of our building at approximately the 78th, 79th, and 80th floors. Our room fell apart at that moment, a complete destruction without an explosion—very strange things. The lights went out, but we were near the window so there was daylight. Again, there was this sort of *thump*, this explosion without fire and flame, a very strange sensation.

There was a twist, if you like, to the building when it got hit, and therefore the plane's hitting explained some things to me later, like why the ceiling fell apart. The ceiling tiles and some of the brackets and so on fell; some air conditioning ducts, speakers, cables, and things like that that were in the ceiling fell. I seem to have a sense that some of the floor tiles even buckled a bit or were moved. Some of the walls, I recall vaguely, were actually torn in a jagged direction rather than up and down. Again perhaps explained by the torque, some of the door frames popped out of the wall and partially fell or fully fell.

For seven to ten seconds there was this enormous sway in the building. It was one way, and I just felt in my heart, *Oh my gosh, we are going over.* That's what it felt like. Now, on windy days prior to that there was a little bit of a sway to the building. You got used to it; you didn't notice it. The window blinds would go *clack clack* as they swung. As I said, for a good seven to ten seconds I thought it was over—horrible feeling—but then the building righted itself. It didn't sway back and forth; it just went one way, it seemed, and then back, and we were stable again.

I was looking at Bobby Coll square in the eyes, and we knew in an instant that it was terrorism. I mean, there wasn't for sure terrorism on people's minds when the first building had been hit. Was it pilot error? Was it instrument error? Or just a one-off suicide? Horrible as it was, you didn't know for certain that it was terrorism. But when the second building got hit you instantly calculated the two of them: terrorism.

The Evacuation

So we knew we were in a difficult situation at that point in time. I fortunately had a flashlight with me, and I'm glad I did. I switched it on, and we started out of the room. Our room was not black with smoke but sort of white with chalky construction dust. It was incredibly dusty and dirty as we made our way out of the room and over some debris that had fallen from the ceiling and so on past the ladies room where I had taken Susan maybe 10 minutes earlier, and we went to this center core, this crossroads in the middle of the building.

At that point, had we gone three or four yards straight ahead to the east, we would have come to Stairway B. I have no idea what condition it was in because we didn't know what had happened, we didn't know where this plane had hit, we didn't know if it was a plane, we didn't know anything other than suddenly we were in chaos and our building had been hit. I could have turned right three yards to Stairway C, closer to the impact point. I had no idea what condition that stairway was in. Miraculously, at random I turned left to Stairway A, which on the floor plate is the farthest from where the impact really was.

So we started down that stairway. We only went three floors. There was a group of seven of us, myself and six others. I remember some of the names. Now, I know everybody at Euro Brokers, but in my mind somehow I blanked out who those other grey shapes were; they were farther up the stairs a bit, not in the light of the flashlight. I do remember Bobby Coll, Kevin York, David Vera, and Ron DiFrancesco.

We met two people that had come up from the 80th floor, a heavy-set woman and by comparison a rather frail male companion of hers, a workmate. She was saying from the landing below, "Stop, stop you've got to go up," and she labored up to join us, moving very slowly; she was such a big woman. She said, "You've got to go up. You can't go down.

There is too much smoke and flames below." I had my flash-light, and I was shining it in each face as people made com-ments, and an argument ensued as to what we should do.

The Rescue

At the same moment as this argument was going on I heard *bang, bang, bang, thump, thump, thump,* "Help! Help! I'm buried. I can't breathe. Is anybody there? Can you help me?," a strange voice coming from within the 81st floor. I heard this voice, and it caused me to lose concentration in this argument that was going on about whether to head up or down. I grabbed Ron by the sleeve, and I said "Come on, Ron. Let's get this fellow."

The fire escape door had blown away from the wall a bit, but we were able to push the dry wall back and step between the door frame and the dry wall, squeeze onto the 81st floor, which was in darkness, but again I had my flashlight. I scanned the room, and I said, "Who's there? Where are you?" He said, "Oh, I can see your light."

What my light beam was showing me was similar to be-ing on a very foggy road at night, because it was white dust everywhere. He said, "No, to the right . . . to the left . . ." In about a minute, Ron and I located his voice. He said, "Can you see my hand?" His hand was sticking out of the wall, or not the wall but this area where he was covered and blocked by some debris. He was waving his hand frantically, and my light picked up his hand. I said, "Okay, see you now."

And at that moment my associate Ron who came down with me was overcome with smoke. He had a gym bag or a briefcase with him, and he was sort of putting it in front of his face in an attempt to filter the air. It clearly wasn't work-ing, and Ron, with eyes shut, backed off the floor. He was almost completely overcome by the smoke.

Again, miraculously, I was in a bubble. I was breathing fine. I was squinting a bit, but I could work, and I struggled to get debris away from Stanley—I found out later his name was Stanley Praimnath; he worked at Fuji Bank.

We got to the point I couldn't do any more work from my

side, and I said, "You've got to jump. You've got to get over this last barrier." Well, he jumped once and fell back down. I said, "Come on, you've got to do this. It's the only way out." I reached in again, and Stanley jumped, and I got him by the collar or the shoulder or somewhere there. He said later that I just pulled him up like Superman. I don't remember having this extraordinary strength, but he says it really did happen that way. I pulled him out and onto me, and we fell in a heap and embraced. It was an exciting moment, it really was.

Now, Ron had gone. He had gone back to the stairway and was not there when we got back to the stairs. The other people had gone up as I left with Ron to go in on the 81st floor. I had this vision of Bobby Coll and Kevin York each with a hand under each elbow of this heavy-set woman starting to ascend the stairs, saying things like, "Come on. We are in this together. We will help you. Relax, we'll be with you." And up they went. And Dave Vera, who had a walkie-talkie, started back up the stairs as well. That's the last I saw of those people.

Now, I didn't know whether Ron had gone up or down, I assumed down because he was with me going down. I learned later that Ron went up; in fact, he went all the way up to the 91st floor. He later told me that he lay on the floor there for 10 minutes until he panicked. He told me, "I had to see my wife. I had to see my kids at all costs. I was gonna make it out." And he went to the stairway and went all the way down, following me, I guess, by five to seven minutes, because I took my time going down the stairway. It was not intentional; it was just that some events happened.

The Descent

So Stanley and I went back to the stairs on the 81st floor, and we began down. The first five floors were difficult, because in certain areas dry wall had been blown off the wall and was lying propped up against the railing. We had to move it, shove it to the side. The sprinkler system had turned on and had started to do something, but it wasn't doing its job as it should, so there was water sloshing down the stairways. It was dark.

Now, the stairways didn't go straight down. There was one particular area around the 78th floor, I think, where you actually came to some strange twists. So we had to figure that out in the darkness, but we made some fortunate decisions. Around the 74th floor, I would say, we broke into what I call fresh air. The lights were on. It was normal conditions. There was not a problem breathing, and there was nobody there, not a soul, just Stanley and me. We were starting to have normal conversation. He was cut and bruised a bit, but he was fine conversing. I think he had his shirt off; he was just in his undershirt.

We continued on down. On the 68th floor, we met one man walking up. The man's name was Jose Marrero. He worked for Euro Brokers for many years. He worked in our security department, and he was also one of our fire marshals. Jose, I learned later, had been with many people of ours all the way down into the 30s and 40s on the stairway and figured, I guess, that he had done his job. Then he heard Dave Vera, who had started down with me, on his walkie-talkie saying that he needed help; he was helping people, could he get help.

So Jose, hero that he was, was walking up, perspiring, carrying his walkie-talkie. He said, "Oh, I can hear Dave above. I'm gonna help." I said, "Jose, Dave's a big boy, he can get out. We've just come through hell to get here. Come on down with us." "No, no, no," he said. "I'll be fine. I can help." Then Jose kept marching up. Jose was about 35 years old and quite fit, but when I passed him he was understandably laboring to climb the stairs. But he kept going. I don't know how high he got or what he found.

Stanley and I continued down until we got to the 44th floor—straight shot, saw nobody. On the 44th floor we went off, because I knew that was one of the sky lobbies in the Trade Center. There were sky lobbies on the 44th and 78th floors. Conditions on the 44th floor were normal other than there was nobody there, except for one—I'm guessing at his age—middle 60s, maybe 70s even, Port Authority security guard who was tending to a Caucasian male lying flat on the floor moaning in pain, with massive head wounds. The security guard was saying, "I need help. My phones don't work, but I need medical attention for this man. I'll stay with him, I'll tend him, but you must promise to get help as soon as you can telephone somebody." Stanley and I said "okay" and went back to the stair.

The Conference Room

We went down again. Nobody on the stairway at all. Easy travel, just the two of us. Lights on, fresh air all the way down to the 31st floor, where we went in at random and got into somebody's office. I don't know whether it was an advertising agency or a lawyer's office; I don't know whose it was. We got into their conference room, and each grabbed a phone.

I called my wife to tell her here's where I am; we'll have this great celebration at home. I hadn't talked to her since about five to nine, I suppose, and this was about 20 to 10. My wife had turned on the TV, and the first thing she had seen was the second plane slam into our building. So she had no idea where I was for that 45-minute stretch. I told her I was fine. Stanley talked to his wife, told her similar news.

I then called 9-1-1—coincidence 9/11—and was put on hold. This was a disturbing thing at the time. I got ahold of them right away and told them about this fellow on the 44th floor that needed medical attention, but they put me on hold. They said, "You must tell your story to somebody higher up the chain" and clicked me off. I'd wait until somebody came on, I'd recite the story, and "Oh, just a minute. You must tell somebody else." I mean, there was something clearly odd about what was going on there. They were answering the phone in a hurry, and I understand now they were completely overwhelmed at the time.

I was asked for a third time to tell somebody else my story, and I just laid down the law. I said, "No. I have given you the details. Here they are one more time," and I wouldn't let that person off the phone. I said, "I'm gonna tell you this once, and then I'm hanging up." I went through the details about the 44th floor, man on the ground, need a medic, need a stretcher, goodbye." I put down the phone. I don't feel badly about that but it was a strange, strange event in the midst of this whole story. We were probably in that conference room for four minutes I would think, and then it was back to the stairs.

The Ground Floor

Now, bear in mind we had no idea that the building was about to fall. We were taking our time. In fact, I said to Stanley at one point, "Hey, let's not go too fast here. I'd hate to break an ankle and have to walk 30 floors or something." So we took our time getting down. We went all the way down, again with nobody on the stairs, not firemen coming up, nobody else evacuating. So all the way down to the Plaza level. We came out by what's known as the "half-price ticket booth," where they sold theater tickets for half price. This was on the north side of the South Tower facing the Plaza.

We came out and stared, awestruck. What we looked at was normally a flowing fountain, vendors with their wagons, business people coming to and from the building, tourists everywhere. It was a beautiful people place, yet this area, several acres I'm sure, was dead; it was a moonscape. It looked like it had been deserted for 100 years, and we had just discovered it.

It was surreal, the whole thing was surreal. We stared at it for 20 or 30 seconds with our jaws dropped, saying, "What is happening here, this is very strange." We went down an escalator that wasn't working—all electricity was off, other than the emergency electricity, I guess, in the stairway—and through some revolving doors, because the women at the bottom of the escalator said to us, "If you're gonna leave the building you have to go this way, through there, and go down to the Victoria Secret shop, turn right, and exit by the Sam Goody store."

We knew where that was, so we walked very casually

down that hallway, down the second hallway, and we were passing firemen and policemen who were going about their business, walking normal speeds. I didn't sense there was panic. It looked like they were under control, doing their job. There were other evacuees like Stanley and me, but there was no running or crowds. It was more or less deserted.

The Street

We got out to the south exit of Four World Trade Center on the southeast corner of the complex. Firemen and policemen stood at the door. One said, "Whoa, wait a minute fellows, if you are gonna cross Liberty Street, you had better go for it. There is debris falling from above." I recall saying, "Should I look up?" He said, "Well, I wouldn't. Just go for it."

I couldn't make myself do that. I crept out under the eaves, and I cautioned a look up this way and that way, and I said, "All right, Stanley, I don't see anything coming. Are you ready?" He said, "Yup," and after one more check, I said, "All right, let's go," and we ran across Liberty Street, which is quite wide at that point, several lanes. There was nobody there. It was very much like a demilitarized zone. There was no traffic. There were some emergency vehicles around but certainly no movement and really not very many people; people were noticeably absent.

Across the road you could see some people standing in doorways protecting themselves from anything that might have been falling. We ran across the street, past the fire hall, which is on the corner, and up another block and caught our breath. There was a deli owner there. I said, "Have you got any water?" He went in and just handed us this water in bottles and said, "Here you go." I said, "Thank you." He said, "In fact, here is a breakfast platter. I don't think anybody is going to be picking that up." And he gave me this great tray with some fresh fruit on it and some sweet rolls. He was a very generous fellow at the time considering the conditions.

I carried this with me another block to the west side of Trinity Church, where we met a couple of ministers. That's when Stanley broke down. He cried to these ministers, "This

man saved my life." He completely broke down. I was overcome with emotion as well, and I said, "You know, Stanley,
you may think I saved your life but I think you saved my
life, too. You got me out of that argument as to whether I
should go up or go down. I'm here, and I'm fine, and it's because of your voice in the darkness that I made it." . . .

It Was Real

We wandered over to the east side of Manhattan, the East
River. Stanley gave me his business card, and thank good-
ness he did, because in the crowd that was walking, he and
I suddenly got parted. He just disappeared into the crowd. I
yelled and looked and walked back and forth but he was
gone. I was very grateful I had his business card at that
point, because I knew that he was real. My initial thought
was, Whoa, this was an angel; this didn't happen. It was a
strange feeling that slipped over me. But, hey, I had his business card, so I knew he was real. . . .

That's my story. It was a long, horrific day, but for me it
turned out all right. For many others, I'm deeply saddened
that they aren't here. We lost 61 people in total, some of
whom I think were either caught in elevators coming back
to the office or had come back to the office. We'll never
know for sure whether it was a wingtip and flames that
caused their demise right on the 84th floor in the east side
of the building, where a lot of our traders were, or whether
it was smoke when they went higher, or whether it was the
collapse of the building. Nonetheless, as I say, we lost 61
friends—dear friends that we worked with and laughed with
for years.

Trapped in the North Tower

Dave Lim

> Dave Lim is a police officer in the canine unit of the Port
> Authority of New York and New Jersey Police Department.
> His dog, Sirius, was a bomb-detection dog. At the time of the
> first attack, on Tower One, Lim and Sirius were in Lim's
> office in the basement of Tower Two. Lim left Sirius in his
> kennel when he went to help with the rescue effort in the
> other tower. Lim was in Tower One when Tower Two col-
> lapsed, but he believed Sirius was safe because he was in the
> basement. Then Tower One collapsed and Lim was stuck in a
> fourth-floor stairwell with other police and fire officers for
> several hours before they were rescued. Sirius was the only
> police dog killed during the attacks. His remains were found
> January 22, 2002, and were removed draped under an Ameri-
> can flag. The flag was displayed at his memorial service,
> which was held April 24 after all the Port Authority officers
> killed in the collapse had been memorialized.

My office is in the first basement level of the south
tower, where I have my desk and a cage for my dog,
Sirius. He is a yellow Lab retriever, and he might have been
the brightest dog I ever have seen, which is why I named
him after the brightest star in the Canis Major constellation.
He is a great dog, trained in explosives detection, and he is
also the family pet. Our job is to check every truck that
comes in and around the building for explosives.

Excerpted from *Report from Ground Zero*, edited by Dennis Smith (New York: Viking,
2002). Copyright © 2002 by Dennis Smith. Reprinted by permission of the publisher.

I jump when I hear the plane go into the north tower. It sounds like a bomb has gone off, and I say to the dog, "Maybe they got one by us, Sirius."

Dead Bodies

I leave the dog there, and run over to the north tower. I see a dead body next to the bandstand where they have set up for a noon concert, and I call it in on my radio. "WTC, I have a DOA [Dead On Arrival] on the plaza."

And WTC radios back, "Is that DOA confirmed?"

I am about to answer when another body lands just fifty feet from me with a very loud noise, [and again] I jump. I look over and see that the skin has been forced away from the flesh. "There is another," I say, as I run into the lobby of the north tower and up the B stairs. I see people coming down, and I keep saying, "Go down, down is good." On the twenty-seventh floor I come across a large man in a wheelchair. He will be difficult to assist, but I call it in on the radio, and proceed up to the forty-fourth floor, where there is a sky lobby, a large, open space where people change elevator banks. I look out of the window and see this huge fireball rushing out of the north side of the south tower. This is the second plane.

Suddenly, all the windows on the east side of my sky lobby are blown out by the concussion, and the wave hits me and several people around me, and we are thrown to the ground. We get up and start down the stairs immediately. I go from floor to floor and try to make a quick search, but I don't stop at any floor where I see firefighters because I know they are searching.

The Buildings Collapse

Somewhere between the fortieth floor and the twentieth I feel the building shake, and then the radio says that the south tower has collapsed. Obviously, if that building collapsed, we are now in a lot more danger. There is a call for immediate evacuation. I am thinking about Sirius in the south tower, but I think he must be safe because he is in the basement, and the collapse would be above. So, I get down to the fifth floor and there I meet Billy Butler and Tommy Falco from Ladder 6. They have a woman named Josephine with them. I begin to give them a hand carrying her, and then the building starts to collapse.

It is an incredible sound, like the combination of an oncoming locomotive and an avalanche, with a huge windstorm right behind. Everything is shaking, like in an earthquake, and it feels like an eternity, that it is never going to stop. I know what I am in, and I just want to see my wife and two children again.

But now there is a dead silence, and it stays dead until I hear someone begin to take a roll call. "Who is that?" I ask.

"Captain Jonas," I hear. We cannot see anything.

There is a man, Mike Meldrum of Ladder 6, sitting on the landing. He has been hit hard, and has a concussion. He is pretty woozy, and he ties his personal rope around his waist, and I tie it onto a handrail to keep him stabilized in case he falls. Mike is asking for something to drink, anything, because he has all the debris and dust in his lungs. I guess we all do. Amazingly, I find a can of soda on the steps, and I pass it to him. He takes a big swig.

I hear a radio message from Chief Prunty, who is a few floors below us. It is a very sad thing to hear this. "Listen," he says, "you have to get here quick." The firefighters try to get down to him, but the whole second floor is completely entombed, and there is no way to get down to him.

We smell jet fuel, and I wonder now, having survived this, is everything just going to explode into fire? I have been on the job for twenty-one years, and I just think in terms of emergencies.

We climb up to the sixth floor, and there the smoke and dust begins to clear, and suddenly there is a little light, and then a big light, and I realize it is the sun. We seem to be on top of the collapse, if that is possible. I say to anyone, "What are the chances that we have survived this?"

Chief Picciotto is there, and he answers, "One in a billion, Officer," he says. "One in a billion."

I try my wife, Diane, on my cell phone, and I get through to her. We talk for a while, but she doesn't want the conversation to end. She wants to stay on the phone until she dies or I die, till the end. And I have to convince her to hang up so that I can give the firefighters a chance to call home, too.

Rescue

Captain Jonas has communication with people in the street, and finally we see Lieutenant Rohan come in the distance. Chief Picciotto and Captain Jonas make a rope guideline, and we send Meldrum out first because he is very dizzy and hurt. I go with him, and we have to stop a few times on the climb out, so that Mike can rest and keep it all together. Rohan sends two firefighters to help Josephine and prepare her for the Stokes basket that will carry her out, and he tells another firefighter to show us the way out of the collapse area, [via] the way he came in.

All of a sudden I started to hear gunfire. These rounds popping off, and I think of our enemies. I know they attacked us, and maybe they landed on the beach. Maybe we'll have to fight. I have forty-six rounds on me. And then I realize that the Secret Service has a firing range in the next building. I look at my watch. It is now 3 P.M., and it is the first time I get to see the scene I am in. It reminds me of the war scene in the first *Terminator* movie, everything destroyed. We get led out—it takes a long time and a lot of climbing. The ambulances come to meet us, and sitting in one, I say to Mike, "I have to go get my dog. He's downstairs."

"Good luck," Mike says.

Sirius

I go over to tower one, and there are several cops and firefighters there who will not let me pass. It is too dangerous. I tell them about the dog, and they said I could not try to go down in any case. I had Sirius for eighteen months, and I truly believed he would survive. He's a good dog. He'll just wait there in his cage until somebody comes to get him out. If we could survive, he will survive.

They take me to St. Vincent's Hospital and admit me. I'm beat up, and my breathing isn't right. I can't see. The Port Authority Canine Unit brings my wife and my children, Debra, 14, and Michael, 12, in to visit. This is a very emotional time for me, and I am very happy when I am with them.

After a week, I have to realize that Sirius isn't coming home, and I have to have a long talk with my son, Michael, about that. He has bonded with the dog, and it is a sad time for us to know he won't be coming home, and he won't be there on the small rug by the bed where he sleeps every night. He was a good working dog, and he was a great family pet at home. The rest is history.

People Are Jumping

Conor O'Clery

> Conor O'Clery is a New York City–based reporter for the
> *Irish Times*. His office was just three blocks away from the
> World Trade Center. When he heard the explosion of the first
> plane crashing into the first tower, he ran to his office window
> and watched the building burn. As he stood there, he saw the
> second plane crash into the other tower. The fireball explo-
> sion from the planes immediately incinerated everything in
> its path—desks, chairs, paper, carpet, and humans. It is esti-
> mated the inferno reached 2,000 degrees, hot enough to melt
> steel. Thousands of people were trapped by debris, fire, and
> collapsed walls and stairs, and were unable to get off their
> floors. Rather than succumb to a horrifying death by fire or
> smoke inhalation, many chose to jump to their death. Onlook-
> ers below, such as O'Clery, were horrified by the thought that
> these people would rather fall 1,000 feet to their death than
> remain in the building.

The first bang came at 8.50 A.M., shaking the windows of my 42nd floor office which has a clear view of the two World Trade Centre towers three blocks to the southeast.

I looked out and saw a huge ball of flame and black smoke billowing out of the north-facing side of the nearest tower.

As the smoke cleared a massive hole 10 stories high became visible just below the top 10 floors and flames could be seen encircling the building behind its narrow slit-like windows.

The Second Plane Appears

Ten minutes later a passenger plane appeared from across the Hudson River heading straight for the second tower.

I didn't notice it until the last minute.

It was tilted so that the flight path took it straight towards the second tower.

It hit and simultaneously a gigantic ball of flame emerged from the east side of the second tower as if the plane had crashed right through the heart of the 110-storey building.

Debris fell in chunks onto West Side Highway followed by a blizzard of shards of glass and paper where ambulances and fire engines were beginning to congregate.

Flames began to leap from the side of the Marriott Hotel just across from where the tiny white Greek Orthodox church stands incongruously in a car park.

People by this time were streaming from the bottom floor of the World Trade Centre, which stands on top of a shopping mall and wide marbled corridors containing airline offices, shops, and a subway station.

Some 50,000 people work in the seven-building complex and many would have been in their offices by now.

Tourists would have begun arriving to queue for the lifts to the top of the tower with its famous Windows on the World restaurant and wonderful views over Manhattan.

But they would not have been taken up to the 107th floor observation deck until it opened at 9.30 A.M.

People at the Windows

Watching through binoculars I could see people hanging out of the windows beside and above where the fires were raging.

One man waved a white cloth as he clung to a window strut.

Then a body fell from a window above him with arms and legs outstretched and plummeted some 100 stories onto Vesey Street.

Two other people fell in the succeeding minutes.

I ran down to the streets where office workers and traders, still wearing their red jackets, were milling around.

Some women were screaming "Oh my God, people are jumping, Oh my God."

Some of the residents of my building, where many members of the financial district live, were sobbing uncontrollably. I returned to the office.

As I watched, the top of the second tower suddenly fell outwards onto West Side Highway, the main thoroughfare along the western side of Manhattan which passes right by the World Trade Centre.

Massive jagged pieces of the tower the size of houses crashed onto two fire engines and onto rescue workers on the roadway.

A huge cloud of dust and ashes rose from the impact, enveloping the Embassy Suites Hotel across the highway and the 50-storey buildings of the World Financial Centre which house Merrill Lynch and stands between the towers and the Hudson River promenade.

I shifted my eyes upwards to the first tower that had been hit and was still standing, and saw that several more people had appeared in the upper stories where they had smashed windows.

The man with the white cloth was still there, hanging precariously by one hand with his body out over the abyss.

I wondered why there was no attempt to rescue them by helicopter as part of the roof of the 1,350-foot building was clear of smoke.

But then the tower began to sway slightly and two people fell in quick succession from the windows as if unable to maintain their grip, falling down onto West Side Highway into the dust and smoke from the first collapse.

The Tower Falls

Then the tower simply slid in on itself, imploding with a huge roar, leaving the lift-shaft like a stump of a blasted tree with twisted metal arms.

This time the clouds of dust and smoke were so huge they enveloped the whole of southern Manhattan.

Thousands of tons of rubble fell onto Tobin Plaza, where

open air concerts are sometimes held and onto the annex housing Borders giant book store.

A westerly breeze kept it about a hundred yards from my building. As it cleared, the scene around the towers was like one from a war zone, which it truly was.

The roadway and pavements and bicycle path, all the streets, cars, fire engines, pavements, traffic lights, awnings and police vehicles, were coated with dust. The green park between my building and the towers where kids play American football had been transformed into a grey field, as if covered with a toxic snow.

About 20 cars in the open air car park between it and the disaster scene were on fire.

As the dirty grey and brown smoke cleared around midday I could see that the Marriott Hotel had taken the full force of the falling tower.

All its windows were shattered and long strips of jagged metal hung over the awning.

The wide, covered pedestrian bridge from the mezzanine level of the financial centre and the Winter Gardens, with its palm trees, was a twisted mass of wreckage.

Out on the streets again, people who had been standing aghast in Battery Park by the river were now streaming uptown on foot.

"Go north, head north," shouted a police officer. The police and firemen remained mostly calm but their faces reflected the horror of the certainty that they had just lost many comrades.

Too Horrible to Contemplate

Before the collapse dozens of firemen and police had rushed into the twin towers to try to help with the evacuation.

What had become of them? It was too horrible to contemplate.

Or to think of the thousands of people trying to escape from both towers, executives in suits, receptionists at polished desks, secretaries, traders, messengers, choking in their offices or racing down smoke-filled emergency stairwells below the destruction line.

It was just 10 minutes before nine when the first plane crashed into one of the towers and the offices were undoubtedly all either doing business or preparing for another working day.

The two gift shops at the top and the food court would have been almost ready to open up.

In the mall below thousands at that time of day criss-cross through the wide corridors past designer stores and coffee shops and newspaper vendors.

Shocked and weeping people trotted down Greenwich Street and west Broadway and Broadway with their hands to their eyes, obeying the arm-waving police officers, and fleeing in the direction of uptown.

Others crowded onto the cross-Hudson ferries at the harbour surrounded by the financial centre buildings. The ferries had borne workers from the New Jersey shore to their work in the financial district just two hours before. The clothes of those caught in the explosion of dust were coated with grey, some had dust-covered hair and eyebrows.

Between midday and one o'clock there were three more muffled bangs from the vast area still hidden by thick acrid smoke as more sections of the two towers collapsed.

As the smoke drifted eastwards further scenes of immense destruction came into view: The twisted metal and piles of rubble and crushed dust-shrouded emergency vehicles which filled Vesey Street and West Side Highway.

There among the rubble, coated with dust, were many bodies, some of those who had jumped, and some of firemen caught beneath the heavy, deadly cascade of falling concrete and metal.

Another plane appeared overhead, causing a frisson of panic but it turned out to be a military jet, arriving one assumes to shoot out of the sky any further suicide pilots. It was too late to save downtown Manhattan.

Watching the Towers Fall

Timothy Townsend

When the planes crashed into the two towers of the World Trade Center, debris was scattered on the streets below for blocks around the buildings. People remarked on the papers floating in the air like a ticker-tape parade. But larger and more hazardous debris were also flying through the air. Detritus from the airplane, such as engines, luggage, and pieces of the human passengers, also littered the streets. Timothy Townsend, a financial reporter, saw all this and more as he wandered around the base of the World Trade Center. He also watched, horrified, as people threw themselves out of the buildings in an attempt to escape the fate of being burned to death. Then, he gazed in astonishment and fear as the south tower collapsed in on itself. He and thousands of other spectators fled away from the building to try and escape from the dark cloud of ash, soot, glass, metal, and concrete debris that was hurtling toward them. His attempts to hide from the ash and dust cloud were futile as was his use of his tie to cover his face. When Townsend finally returned home, he realized that when he watched the tower collapse he was witnessing the death of a friend.

The first thing I saw in the parking lot across Liberty Street from the South Tower was luggage. Burned luggage. A couple of cars were on fire. Half a block east, a man who'd been working out in a South Tower fitness club was

From "The First Hours," by Timothy Townsend, www.rollingstone.com, September 11, 2001. Copyright © 2001 by Rolling Stone Magazine. Reprinted with permission.

walking barefoot over shards of glass, wearing only a white towel around his waist; he still had shaving cream on the left side of his face. Bits of glass were falling to the ground like hail. I ventured a block south, away from the towers, and that's when I started seeing body parts. At first, just scattered lumps of mangled flesh dotting the road and its sidewalks, then a leg near the gutter. Someone mentioned a severed head over by a fire hydrant. Hunks of metal—some silver and the size of a fist, others green and as big as toasters—were strewn for blocks south of the buildings. Shoes were everywhere.

The Jumpers

"Oh Jesus," I heard someone say. "They're jumping." Every few moments a body would fall from the North Tower, from about ninety floors up. The jumpers all seemed to come from the floors that were engulfed in flames. Sometimes they jumped in pairs—one just after the other. They were up so high, it took ten to twelve seconds for each of them to hit the ground. I counted.

What must have been going through their minds, to choose certain death? Was it a decision between one death and another? Or maybe it wasn't a decision at all, their bodies involuntarily recoiling from the heat, the way you pull your hand off a hot stove.

Moments later, a low metallic whine, quickly followed by a high-pitched whoosh, came out of the south. I looked up to see the white belly of an airplane much closer than it should have been. The South Tower of the Trade Center seemed to suck the plane into itself. For an instant it looked like there would be no trauma to the building—it was as if the plane just slipped through a mail slot in the side of the tower, or simply vanished. But then a fireball ballooned out of the top of the building just five blocks from where we stood.

People were running south down the West Side Highway toward Battery Park—the southern tip, the end, of Manhattan—and west toward the Hudson River. I ran with the crowd that veered toward the river, looking back over my

shoulder at the new gash in the Trade Center. Once relatively safe among the tree-lined avenues of Battery Park
City, people hugged each other and some cried.

After about ten minutes, a wave of calm returned to the
streets. Police were trying to get the thousands of people
south of the Word Trade Center off the West Side Highway,
east to the FDR Drive, over the Brooklyn Bridge. And still
people were throwing themselves out of the North Tower:
You could see suit jackets fluttering in the wind and
women's dresses billowing like failed parachutes.

The First Tower Falls

But about five minutes later, a sharp cracking sound mo-
mentarily replaced the shrill squeal of sirens, and the top half
of the South Tower imploded, bringing the entire thing down.
It was the most frightened I've ever been. Screaming and
sprinting south toward Battery Park, we all flew from the dark
cloud that was slowly funneling toward us. At that moment,
I believed two things about this cloud. One, that it was made
not just of ash and soot, but of metal, glass and concrete; and
two, that soon this shrapnel would be whizzing by—and perhaps through—my head. A woman next to me turned to run.
Her black bag came off her shoulder and a CD holder went
flying, sending bright silver discs clattering across the ground.
An older man to my right tripped and took a face-first dive
across the pavement, glasses flying off his face.

In the seconds, minutes and hours following the World
Trade Center attacks, hundreds—maybe thousands—of ordinary people would find their best selves and become heroes. And then there were the rest of us, running hard, wanting only to live and to talk to someone we loved, even if it
meant leaving an old guy lying in the street, glasses gone, a
cloud of death and destruction creeping up on him.

I'd always wondered what I'd do in a life-or-death situation. Until that moment, I'd believed I'd do the right thing,
would always help the helpless, most likely without regard
for my own well-being. All across lower Manhattan at that
moment, people were making similar decisions, so many of

them so much more critical than mine. September 11th, 2001, at 9:45 A.M. was not my finest moment. As I turned back to help, I saw two younger guys scoop the fallen man up, and we all continued running south.

Nowhere to Go

After about three blocks, I hid for a moment behind a large Dumpster on the west side of the street. But when I looked back toward the towers, I could see that my Dumpster was no match for the cloud, and I took off again. I ran the last few blocks into Battery Park, where the cloud finally did catch up with the thousands of us fleeing it. I could see only a few feet in front of me, and so I followed the silhouettes I could make out. Because Battery Park is the tip of the island, it wasn't much of a surprise that the crowd would wind up dead-ending at the water. When it happened, the people in the front panicked. So they turned around, screamed, and ran back toward us in a stampede. We had nowhere to go—there were thousands of people behind us and hundreds coming back the other way.

As the crowd doubled back on itself, I jumped over a wrought-iron fence and landed in a flower bed. I stayed down for a second, thinking I'd wait out the panic low to the ground. But then I felt other people jumping the fence and landing near me. Thinking I was about to be trampled, I got up and ran behind a nearby tree. In a minute or two the panic subdued, and I hopped back over the fence and onto a park path. But now the air was heavier with debris and there was no clear path out of the park. I took off my tie and wrapped it around my face. People were coughing and stumbling. Some were crying, others screaming. It was difficult to breathe or even keep my eyes open.

Soon, there was another wave of calm and quiet, and the ash that fell from the sky and settled on the grass and trees gave the park the peaceful feel of a light evening snowfall. Eventually, I found a path that led me out to the east side of the Battery area, and I followed a crowd to the FDR. Thousands participated in the exodus up the highway and into

Brooklyn. It was now just past ten, and we looked like refugees. In a way, we were. My tie wasn't doing much good against the ash, so I took off my shirt and tied it around my head. We walked in the falling gray dust for fifteen minutes, still hacking, and rubbing our eyes. Then the cloud broke, and, covered in soot, we were in the sunlight again. There wasn't a lot of talking. Some walked in groups, desperately trying to stay together. Others walked alone, crying out the names of friends, co-workers or loved ones from whom they'd been separated.

Watching a Friend Die

At 10:25, as I was getting ready to cross the bridge, another cracking sound came out of the west. We looked behind us and to the left to see the remaining tower collapse. Soon, that ash reached the Manhattan foot of the Brooklyn Bridge, and the bridge was closed. Three hours later, I was finally back in my apartment in Brooklyn. It was nearly one o'-clock. There was a thin layer of ash all over my kitchen from the blast. I made my phone calls and cried with my fiancee. Then I called some friends who'd left messages, checking on me. I called my friend Sully in Boston, and we went through the list of names of our friends who worked in the financial district. I was one of the last to be accounted for. When we'd gotten through most of the names—Sims, Kane, T-Bone, Molloy—Sully said, "It's not all good news. Beazo called his wife from high up in the second building to say he was OK, but she hasn't heard from him since it fell." Beazo—Tom Brennan to those he didn't go to high school or college with—still hasn't been heard from.

As it turns out, when I was watching that tower fall, I was watching my friend die. His wife was at home, in their brand-new house in Westchester County, amid their still boxed-up life. She'd already turned off the TV when Beazo's building collapsed. Their seventeen-month-old daughter is too young to have seen the images of her father's death, but someday—maybe on a distant anniversary of September 11th when each network commemorates the tragedy—I'm sure she'll be able to see it, along with her little brother or sister who is due in two months. I hung up with Sully and turned on the television to see what I had seen. Places where I once ate lunch or shopped for a sweater or bought stamps were now buried under piles of concrete and metal, as were thousands of people—some of whom I probably rode the subway with every day. One of whom was my friend.

Since then, I've been freakishly fine, given what I'd seen. Maybe it's because I realize how lucky I was—my experience was like Christmas morning compared to what other people went through. Maybe it's because I lack the imagination, or the will, to realize the scope of what I'd seen. But sadness works in bizarre ways. The second night after the attack, I sat in front of the news, alone with my eighth or ninth beer, and I listened to a report about NFL officials considering a postponement of the second week of games. I thought about what a nice gesture that would be, and I cried and cried.

A Burn Victim at the World Trade Center

Greg Manning

> Most of the forty thousand people who worked at the World
> Trade Center made it out alive with few or only minor injuries.
> A small percentage, however, suffered severe burns from the
> fireball that followed the explosion of jet fuel and combustibles
> in the buildings. In the following essay, Greg Manning talks
> about the injuries his wife, Lauren, a senior vice president and
> partner at Cantor Fitzgerald, suffered from the crash.
>   Lauren Manning was just entering the lobby of Tower One
> when the plane crashed into the building. A fireball shot
> down and out of the elevator shaft and engulfed Lauren. Lau-
> ren ran from the building into the street, where two passers-
> by helped put out the flames. One of the strangers went with
> her to the hospital and called Greg to tell him what happened
> to his wife. Lauren suffered severe burns over 80 percent of
> her body and at one time, her chances of surviving her burns
> were only 15 percent. But she did pull through. Greg Man-
> ning began writing daily e-mails to family and friends telling
> them about Lauren's progress and setbacks. He later com-
> bined his e-mails into a book, *Love, Greg and Lauren*, from
> which this essay is excerpted. Greg Manning is a director of
> information sales and marketing at Euro Brokers, which was
> also based in the World Trade Center.

As midnight came on September 11, 2001, I stood at my
wife's bedside in the William Randolph Hearst Burn

Excerpted from *Love, Greg and Lauren*, by Greg Manning (New York: Bantam, 2002).
Copyright © 2002 by Gregory P. Manning. Reprinted by permission of the publisher.

Center at New York–Presbyterian Hospital. Webs of plastic tubing fed her intravenous fluids and medications. Over the next twenty-four hours she would receive approximately twenty liters—forty-two pounds—of fluids to replace those she was losing through her wounds. She was heavily sedated and would remain in this drug-induced sleep for weeks. She was on a ventilator to support her breathing; there was a feeding tube in her nose. Her body was wrapped in white gauze, and she was draped in sheets and blankets to keep her warm. At 8:48 that morning, she had been burned over 82.5 percent of her body as she entered the lobby of 1 World Trade Center.

At 8 that morning she had been a vibrant, athletic, and beautiful woman, decisive and demanding and the picture of health.

At about 8:30 she had breezed through our living room telling me how she'd solved a scheduling problem that morning, making business calls that delayed her normal departure about fifteen minutes. She lingered in the hallway, saying good-bye to our ten-month-old son, Tyler, and then she headed off to work, going downstairs and hailing a cab to take her to the World Trade Center, where she was (and is) a senior vice president, partner, and director of global data sales for Cantor Fitzgerald.

Looking at the Devastation

Less than twenty minutes later, listening to the "Imus in the Morning" program as I was about to leave for work, I heard Imus break in and say, "What's this? A plane hit the World Trade Center?"

I ran to our terrace, which looks down Manhattan's West Street toward the twin towers, and saw a vast hole billowing black smoke from the top of Tower One. I could see that the plane had hit at or just below Cantor Fitzgerald's offices and that the impact had been huge. I tried to persuade myself that Lauren, that anyone at Cantor, could still be alive. I kept calling her telephone numbers but her office line was busy and her cell phone wasn't ringing. I paced the apartment, pounding the wall and calling her name, then watched as the second plane hit Tower Two, seemingly right at the 84th floor, my office at Euro Brokers.

I felt like the man on a battlefield who leaves his unit for a moment, only to look back as it is blown up before his eyes. Friends and family kept calling our apartment to make sure we were all right. I could not say whether Lauren was alive; I was almost certain she was dead.

But she wasn't.

Severely Burned

Arriving at the World Trade Center, she'd heard a whistling sound, entered the lobby to investigate, and been met by an explosive fireball. She ran outside in flames. A bond salesman over at the World Financial Center saw her and two others as they ran from the building, raced across West Street, and put out the flames that were consuming her. Lauren was lucid enough to tell him her name and our phone number. People had fled and there was no one else around for blocks. As heavy pieces of steel debris fell from a thousand feet above them, he stayed with Lauren until the ambulance came.

At 9:35 our phone rang once and went silent. A moment later it rang again. A breathless voice said, "Mr. Manning, I'm with your wife. She's been badly burned but she's going to be OK. We got her in an ambulance." The phone cut off before he could tell me where she was being taken. I was to learn later that the caller was a bond trader. His buddy, the bond salesman, had just saved Lauren's life.

Lauren's parents called from Savannah, Georgia; they literally dropped the phone when I told them the news, got in their car, and took off for New York.

Twenty minutes later a nurse called to tell me Lauren was at St. Vincent's Hospital, eight blocks away. Fighting tears, not knowing what to expect, I made my way there through the stunned crowds headed north on Hudson Street. At one point I turned around and saw Tower One wreathed in black smoke. I did not realize Tower Two had already come down.

At the Hospital

I entered St. Vincent's moments before it was closed to all but patients and medical personnel. I found Lauren in a bed on the 10th floor, all but her face covered in white sheets. She looked normal, though as if she had a deep tan, but her eyebrows had been burned off and her beautiful blond hair was charred.

The first thing she said was "Get me to a burn unit."

Why the Towers Fell

Seven months after the attacks on the World Trade Center, a panel of engineering experts put together by the American Society of Civil Engineers released a report explaining the causes behind the collapse of the twin towers. The final report confirmed an early theory about why the towers fell: The heat generated by the fireball explosions and subsequent fire caused the steel support beams to soften and sag. The weakened beams could no longer support the tremendous weight of the floors, causing the building to pancake.

Fire was the main reason the towers fell, many engineers surmised shortly after the attacks. Or, more precisely, the intense heat generated by thousands of gallons of aviation fuel caused the towers' steel superstructure to bend and buckle. Given the tremendous weight of the floors above the impact zones, we were told, the weakening of so much structural steel inevitably led the buildings to pancake downward.

After viewing and reviewing all the film footage of the events and investigating the ruins for months—particularly the steel remnants from the floors that were directly hit by the planes—members of the [American Society of Civil Engineers] panel agree with the instant analysts. Heat and weakened steel were the principal causes of the structural failure.

But it wasn't the jet fuel itself that generated prolonged temperatures of more than 1,000 degrees Fahrenheit, the experts found. Rather, said one, the airplane fuel was like lighter fluid, instantaneously igniting everything in its path—desks, chairs, papers, books, phones, carpets, com-

Then she said, "Greg, I was on fire. I ran out. I prayed to die. Then I decided to live for Tyler and for you." She asked me to apply balm to her blistered lips. Her pain grew and she begged for morphine. She became less aware. Her face began to swell. They transferred her to a private room and asked me to step out. For the next two hours the nurses dressed her wounds.

At 5 that afternoon, Dr. Edmund Kwan, a plastic surgeon

---

puters, humans—to create two massive caldrons in the sky.

Furthermore, systems designed to prevent, retard and extinguish fires were severely affected by the force of the impact. Spray-on fireproofing was instantly dislodged from steel columns, beams and trusses, rendering them even more vulnerable to the extraordinary heat. Water storage containers, sprinkler systems and pipes were damaged or destroyed, making them useless.

As we all know by heart, the South Tower was the second to be hit but the first to fall. This is because, the engineers concluded, the Boeing 767 jet that was crashed into its north facade was traveling faster than the plane that sought out the North Tower, it impacted at an angle that destroyed more exterior columns, and it came in lower, thus greatly increasing the weight the remaining structure had to bear.

Given the intense heat, say the engineers, there was no chance the building would remain upright. As one researcher comments tersely, "Less than a quarter-hour after impact, all the conditions for the South Tower collapse were in place."

Not that the North Tower had a chance, either. It lasted longer simply because fewer exterior columns were taken out in the initial impact. However, unlike the South Tower crash, that affecting the North Tower damaged a substantial number of steel columns in the central core of the building. Thus, this skyscraper collapsed in a slightly different manner—its core disintegrated, and the building came down with eerie precision.

Benjamin Forgey, "Fire and Steel: Engineers Tell 'Why the Towers Fell,'" *Washington Post*, April 30, 2002.

affiliated with St. Vincent's and New York–Presbyterian, se-
cured Lauren a bed in the Burn Center and ordered her sedated and intubated to protect against respiratory arrest during the transport. The ambulance driver headed across 14th
Street, up on FDR Drive closed to all but emergency vehicles, and rolled to a stop in the hospital's ambulance bay.
Within minutes we were in the Burn Center on the 8th floor.
Lauren was wheeled to a glass-walled room and doctors and
nurses surrounded her bed. Someone led me to the waiting
room and I sagged into a chair.

Keeping Vigil

The hours passed. With the city locked down, home seemed
far away, unreachable. Joyce, Tyler's nanny, stayed with him
that night as I dozed on the floor of the waiting room just
down the hall in case I was called to Lauren's bedside. My
friend Bill Fisher kept the vigil with me. Members of other
patient families slept there too, in chairs or on cots. Lauren's
mother and father arrived at noon on Wednesday. They
would stay in our apartment for the next three months and
be there for Lauren and Tyler. Lauren's sister came in from
New Jersey and her brother drove up from North Carolina.
I asked my own family in Florida—my mother and father
and sister—to remain at home; I did not have a place for
them to stay if they came, and I promised to keep them continually posted on Lauren's condition.

On Thursday evening, a gray-haired man in a white coat
met with us in the waiting room. He was Dr. Roger Yurt, the
medical director of the Burn Center, Lauren's doctor in the
pages that follow. In a calm voice he described what she was
up against. The first seventy-two hours were the resuscita-
tion phase, during which she was receiving an extraordinary
quantity of fluids to replace those her body was dumping. If
she survived this phase, Dr. Yurt would perform numerous
grafts in the ensuing weeks to close her wounds and control
her injury. Only after she was "closed" would she be out of
danger; until then, infection would be a constant threat.

The prognosis was bleak, but the meeting with Dr. Yurt

brought me the first twinge of hope. If there was anyone on earth who could save her, I thought, he was the one.

Late Saturday night, September 15, another critical patient, who had been brought in at the same time as Lauren, died, reducing by one the cadre of bereft and shattered families who had bonded in the waiting room since Tuesday. Dr. Palmer Bessey, Dr. Yurt's associate director, had to deliver the news to the patient's family, and as I was leaving the Burn Center that night he looked up and told me, "She's hanging in there pretty well." He paused. "She's going to get sicker before she gets better." He paused again, then said with quiet ferocity, "But we're going to do everything we can to pull her through. I don't want those bastards to get another person."

In the early afternoon of Sunday, September 16, I was told that Lauren's chances were less than 50-50, probably far less. (I was later to learn they were about 15 percent.) I found solace with a rabbi who was in the waiting room visiting another patient. He was not on the hospital staff, but at my request he came in to pray by Lauren's bedside so that she might hear the holy language and know that we were praying for her.

That night, another World Trade Center burn patient died.

Chapter 2

Rescue and Recovery

Chapter Preface

For the firefighters stationed near the World Trade Center, the call of a fire in Tower One was not unusual; in fact, they responded to fire alarms at the towers on a daily basis. However, the extent of the fire on September 11, 2001, was far beyond ordinary. Entire floors were on fire. And within twenty minutes, both towers were on fire. The buildings' design—with lots of open space on each floor and no interior support columns—allowed the fires to burn freely with no firewalls to slow their progress. Observers reported that the smoke from the fires was black, indicating that the fire was provided with lots of fuel. The smoke turned white as it rose into the air, which meant the fire was intensely hot. Of course, no one realized at the time that each crash's impact blew off the fire-retardant material on the steel girders or that burning jet fuel got the fires so hot that the towers' steel support beams started to melt, weakening the entire structures and allowing them to collapse.

The firefighters rushed to the scene and immediately set up command posts in the buildings' lobbies to direct personnel to the appropriate spots for their duties. Each of the towers was 110 stories tall. In Tower One, the plane crashed into floors ninety-four through ninety-eight; in Tower Two, the plane crashed lower—between the seventy-eighth and eighty-fourth floors. The firefighters knew they had a long climb ahead of them as they entered the stairwells, bringing all their equipment with them. They carried hoses, oxygen tanks, masks, axes, ropes, and more, rescue equipment that weighed sixty or more pounds per person.

Although Tower Two was the second tower to be hit, it was the first tower to fall, collapsing within an hour of the crash. The people inside the building had little or no warning that the building was about to fall. Thousands of people inside Tower Two were saved, though, because they began to evacuate their building as soon as they saw that Tower One had been hit. Many of those who waited to evacuate until the building was attacked did not make it out of the building in time and were killed when the tower collapsed. The workers, firefighters, and rescue personnel inside Tower One were a little luckier; they still had about thirty minutes to escape from the building before their tower collapsed.

Almost 3,000 people died at the World Trade Center, although initial estimates were much higher. Included in that number are 403 rescue workers: 343 New York firefighters, 37 officers from the Port Authority of New York and New Jersey Police Department, and 23 New York City police officers. The death toll could have been much worse. Approximately 50,000 people worked in each building, but the planes hit early in the morning before many workers were at their desks. In addition, the observation deck was not open yet for tourists. New York City mayor Rudy Giuliani expressed the feelings of many when he said that, whatever the final number of people killed, it would be "more than we can bear."

Saving Josephine

Jay Jonas

The New York Fire Department's engine and ladder companies have different responsibilities when fighting fires. The engine company puts out the fires with water hoses; the ladder company is responsible for entering the building and rescuing people inside if necessary. Jay Jonas is the captain of New York Fire Department's Ladder 6 company, which has about twenty-five firefighters.

After the alarm sounded for the fire at the World Trade Center, Jonas and his company entered Tower One, the first tower to be hit by a hijacked airplane. When the unit got to the twenty-seventh floor, the other tower collapsed and they knew it was time to evacuate the building. On their way down the stairs, Jonas and his men encountered a woman named Josephine who, due to problems with her feet, walked very slowly. They were determined to stay with her, however, until they got her out of the building. When the unit got to the fourth floor, Josephine, who had walked down from the seventy-second floor, said she could not walk any further. The firefighters attempted to find some way to carry her down the last few flights of stairs when the building collapsed. When the dust finally settled, Jonas and his men were unhurt. They saw the sun shining through a hole in the stairwell and realized that was their way out. After several hours, Jonas's team and Josephine were all rescued. Many firefighters perished in the collapse, and Jonas believes that if he and his men had not stopped to help Josephine, they would not have made it out alive. His narrative of those harrowing hours follows.

I'd come downstairs after getting cleaned up for the day tour. I worked the night before. I shaved and had gotten dressed, and I was in the kitchen having a bowl of Wheaties and a cup of coffee. The guys keep telling me I should call the Wheaties company because I must hold the record. . . .

All of a sudden we hear this loud boom, and I say, "What the heck was that?" It sounded like a big truck driving off the Manhattan Bridge, which is only about a block away from the firehouse.

And then, my housewatchman starts banging on the intercom and yelling into the intercom. "A plane just crashed, a plane just crashed into the World Trade Center." So we go running out the front of the firehouse, and I'm standing on Canal Street, and I can see the black smoke wafting over, and I said, "Oh, my God."

A Catastrophic Emergency

I keep my bulky gear in the office, which is right off the housewatch, and as I'm pulling on my bunker pants I hear on the department radio, "Engine 10 transmitting a third alarm and a 1060 signal [a catastrophic emergency, like a plane or train crash]."

By the time we get on the fire trucks and are heading out the door, our alarm kicked in. The teleprinter starts going off. Both of our companies are second-alarm units there, so I knew we weren't jumping the gun. As we head down Canal Street, right by the Manhattan Bridge, I have a panoramic view of Lower Manhattan, and I can't believe what I am seeing. The top twenty floors of the World Trade Center are on fire. From that time of me sitting in the kitchen to getting my gear on, and us pulling out of the firehouse, there are twenty floors of fire? What did that take? All of thirty-five to forty-five seconds? I can't believe what I am seeing; it is something out of Hollywood. I've worked in the Bronx. I've worked in Harlem. I've worked on the Lower East Side. I've seen some unbelievable fires in Chinatown, and this is the most amazing thing I'd ever seen. I just yelled to the back of the truck, "Buckle up. We're going to work."

We get to West Street, park the truck, and begin gathering all of our equipment. We're right by the north pedestrian bridge that goes across West Street by Vesey Street.

We're keeping an eye out because there is stuff that is crashing near our truck, big pieces of the building coming off. So we're all seeking shelter under this footbridge, and once we get everything gathered, I turn to my guys and say, "All right, is everybody ready?"

"Yeah," they answer in unison.

I look for a time when I don't see anything falling and I say, "Okay, run!"

Reporting In

And we all sprint to the front of the building. We make it to the lobby. The first thing I see there is two badly burned people, right at the lobby entrance door. I also see that people were starting to come to take care of them. There might be a thousand people upstairs that we have to take care of. I report in to Battalion Chief Joe Pfeifer.

Deputy Chief Pete Hayden was there already, and a couple of officers were in front of me. So, I am waiting my turn in line, waiting to get my orders. I see Paddy Brown from 3 Truck who says "Jay, just come on upstairs; they're just going to send you upstairs."

"No," I say. "Let me check in. Let me get on paper that I'm here."

That was the last time I saw Paddy Brown.

I report in, and just as I'm about to get my orders we hear another loud explosion. I'm not sure what this is, whether it was a few tanks blowing up on our floor, or what. But a guy comes running into our building and said a second plane just hit the second tower. I looked at Chief Hayden, and he says "Jay, just go up, and do the best you can."

I say, "All right, chief."

So we knew that things had radically changed from "Oh, what a horrible accident," to "Oh, my God, they're trying to kill us." I saw it. I am standing next to Jerry Nevins, from Rescue 1, when the plane hit. Terry Hatton is there, Dave

Weiss, all those guys and we just look at each other, and Nevins says, "Oh, man, we're going to be lucky if we survive this."

The Walk Up

I am not thinking collapse. I am thinking eighty stories up, for I have in the back of my mind that we have to make the eightieth floor before we will hit anything major. I figure there will be fuel dropping down, and vapors. I figure that will be when we will start hearing things. "This is going to be a long climb," I say to my men, "and I know it's going to be hard, but that's what we're doing."

Maybe a lower bank of elevators is working that might take us to the fifteenth floor. But I'm not comfortable with that, especially after seeing the people in the lobby that are burned. So that's not a good option.

There is a line of firemen waiting to get into the big stairway. We jump on line and start heading up. I tell the guys, "We're going to take frequent breaks, so we have something left when we get to the upper floors. We're going to rest every ten floors, catch your breath for a little bit, and then we'll push on."

Civilians on the Way Down

We immediately start encountering civilians coming down. They are to our left and we were on the right. It is enough for two people to be comfortable side by side. Every once in a while we stop a civilian trying to come down in the middle. I say, "Stop, stay to your right, and this way everything will work."

For the most part the civilians are very calm. They are on every floor where there is a vending machine, breaking into them, and taking out bottles of Poland Spring water to give to us. That was terrific.

We are staying nice and hydrated on the way up. Every once in a while we see somebody who is burned coming down, but I can't believe how remarkably calm they are. And they are shouting out words of encouragement to us.

"God bless you," and "You guys are remarkable."

We just keep going up, and up. We meet a member from Engine Company 9 who is having chest pains, so we stop, and we take care of him until his company gets with him.

Going up a little farther we find a fireman from Squad 18 who is also having chest pains, and we stop to take care of him quickly.

We move on again. We get to the twenty-seventh floor. I am ecstatic that everybody has stayed together. Each floor in this building is like an acre.

"This is the mother of all high-rise buildings," I say, "and I can't afford to be looking for you guys. So stay together."

An Earthquake Rumble

When we get to the twenty-seventh floor, I'm missing two guys. I tell my other guys to stand fast, and I go down to look for the other two. They got separated due to the civilians coming down, and I find them. So we are all on the twenty-seventh floor, and taking a quick break. I notice that I am no longer seeing civilians. I'm on the twenty-seventh floor with Andy Fredericks from Squad 18 and Billy Burke, the captain of Engine 21. And all of a sudden we hear the rumble, an earthquakelike rumble, and the loud rush of air like a loud jet engine kind of a thing. I look at Billy Burke and say, "Go check those windows, and I'll check these windows." We ran our separate ways, and then came back.

"Is that what I thought it was?" I ask.

"Yeah," Billy answers. "The other building just collapsed."

I just look at my guys now, and say, "It's time for us to go home."

If that one could go, this one could go. As we are leaving, one of my men wants to ditch the roof rope, but I say no, we might need that. We don't know what we might encounter on the way down.

The Way Back Down

We start heading down. There is no immediate call for evacuation of our building, at least I don't hear one, and I am a little nervous heading down. Are we doing the right thing? This is a hard climb up, and I would hate to cover the same territory twice if there is no evacuation.

But I say to myself, *This is not good,* and we just have to get out of here. I realize right away that our situation is pretty grave and that we have to get a move on.

We are in stairway B, and somewhere around the twentieth floor we run into Josephine Harris.

Tommy Falco and Billy Butler find her on the stairs. She can barely walk because she has a serious case of fallen arches or something. She has already walked one step at a time down from the seventy-second floor. Falco says, "Captain, what do you want to do with her?"

We will have to bring her with us, I think. Tommy Falco and Billy are big football linebacker types, and I told them to keep with her. But she was very slow.

Somewhere close to the twentieth floor, I run into Chief Picciotto. I am surprised. He and I have been friends for a long time. We are in the same study group. We socialize together. But I work in Chinatown, and he works on the Upper West Side, so chances of us running into each other are pretty remote.

"Hey, Rich, how are you doing?"

"Jay, all right," he says, and starts heading down with us.

I see Chief McGovern's aide, from the 2nd Battalion, Faustino Apostol. I know him pretty well, for he drives me whenever I am working as acting battalion chief. I look at him and say, "Faust, let's go. It's time to go."

He answers, "That's okay. I'm waiting for the chief."

So he is just standing in his post. He doesn't want to abandon his boss.

As we are going down, I see a few guys from Ladder Company 5 taking care of a man who is having chest pains. They are on a landing, and I know the officer, Mike Warchola.

I say, "Mike, let's go. It's time to go."

He said, "That's all right, Jay. You got your civilians, we got ours. We'll be right behind you."

We are moving down very slowly. A few times we stop to

let other firefighters go past us. One company that passes us is Engine 28. I used to be in that firehouse as a lieutenant.

When we get to the tenth floor, I think that I am glad we brought the rope because it will reach the sidewalk from here. I say to the guys, "Well, we can single slide with the rope now if we have to."

The Fourth Floor

Finally we get the to the fourth floor, and Josephine is saying she can't go any farther. So the guys try to keep her spirits up.

I wonder now if I am getting a false sense of security. Maybe this building is not going to collapse because I look at my watch, and it's been almost twenty-three minutes now since the other building collapsed. I say to the guys, "Well, maybe this isn't going to come down."

But now Josephine falls to the floor, and she is crying. She says, "I can't walk anymore." Meantime, other firefighters are passing us by. We stop to deal with her for a little while, but finally I say, "We gotta get moving."

The Collapse Starts

The fourth floor door is locked, and I break into it, looking for a sturdy chair. We can throw her in a chair, I think, and we can run with her. But there are no chairs. It's a mechanical equipment room, so there isn't much furniture—one desk with a stenographer's chair that won't do. There are a couple of overstuffed chairs and couches. They won't do either. So I start running back to the stairway, and I'm about six to seven feet away from the stairway door when the collapse starts.

I tried the stairway door, and it wouldn't open. But after a second pull, assisted by a gust of strong wind coming down the stairs, the door flies open. And I dive for the stair. I just crawl up into a ball on the stairway landing, and I wait for something to hit us.

There is unbelievable shaking. Almost like I'm being bounced like a basketball. I am literally bouncing off the floor, like if a train derails and the wheels are hitting the railroad ties. It was that kind of *boom, boom, boom, boom* in a loud succession. It's unbelievable, the sound of these massive steel beams and gutters twisting around you like they were twist ties on the loaf of bread. It is a painfully loud screech of steel all around us. Debris is falling on us like a deluge shower.

As it is collapsing, I think, *This is it. It's over. This is how it ends for me. I'm done.*

I thought of Judy and the kids and that's about it. *This is it. It's over.*

And now the sound stops, dead. Just dead silence. My first thought is, *Oh, man! I can't believe I just survived that.* But it's not like we were in this pristine stairway. All kinds of debris is still whacking us all over the place, and knocks my helmet off. I see a couple of my guys, and it knocks their helmets off. It is like we got mugged, we got beat up pretty good in the stairway, but we didn't get hit with anything that was gonna hurt us seriously. Once the collapse stopped, I start to take a deep breath. We are all coughing and gagging from the dust.

And we can't see anything because of the cloud of dust and smoke.

I give a quick roll call to see who we had. I go through all my guys. I say, "Is Josephine still here?"

"Yup."

"How about Chief Picciotto?" I knew he was in front of us.

"Yeah, he's here."

Trying to Continue Down

My first thought is that we will continue down. There was probably a collapse on the upper floors, and it can't be that the lower floors are too bad because we're still here.

Josephine can't walk, and we will have to move her. I teach rescue classes for the state, and I have gotten my men to carry one-inch tubular webbing—it's a twenty-four-foot piece [with which] you can make a harness and everything else. I said, "Put her into a full body harness, and we'll carry her down the stairs." The guys get down one flight of stairs, and Matt Komoroski, our lowest guy, said, "It's no good. There is no getting out this way."

There are two handholds on this webbing, and they pick up her upper body, and her feet are dragging on the way down. She's going down head first, but there is no getting out.

I am thinking that if our stairway was good, we could just walk right out of the lobby. But this isn't the case. So they bring her back up the stairs, back to where we are. Now I hear the radio begin to squawk. "This is the officer of Ladder 5, Lieutenant Warchola, Mayday, Mayday, Mayday. I am on the twelfth floor, B stairway. I'm trapped, and I'm hurt bad."

And so I picked myself up out of the rubble, and I started climbing up to the fifth floor.

Frustration

I had to move a lot of debris [on the way], but when I got there I couldn't move anymore. It was too big and too heavy; it would take a crane. Which broke my heart. When I first heard him I just thought I could climb up there; I could get to him. I've known Mike Warchola for a long time. I used to carpool with him when I was a fireman. And so I press the transmitting key, and say "Mike. I'm sorry. I can't get to you." This is such a hard thing to say.

At this time we start making radio contact with Chief Richard Prunty. He is just below us, on the first floor. Matt Komoroski was on the second floor along with Lieutenant McGlynn of Engine 39. Mickey Kross of Engine 16 is between us.

Chief Prunty isn't able to get much radio contact on the outside, and I think that because we are a little higher, I am able to make pretty good communications.

Chief Prunty, in the meantime, radios that he's in the stairway, he's hurt bad, and he's pinned. And he is starting to feel dizzy, which is very hard for us because we can't get to him.

It is so frustrating to know that geographically you're not that far away from someone, that he's slipping away, and there's not a thing you can do about it. But [at the time, we had no] concept of what the damage from the outside might look like.

We see a light that, after an hour or more, grows bigger and bigger as the smoke lifts. There's a small hole in the stairway where I am on the fourth floor. And I can see out. But all I see is a mountain of steel and the big dust cloud.

From where we came in the stairway, I know looking out that wall is east, and I know exactly geographically where I am in the building. I'm not sure if there are 106 floors above me, but there's got to be something dangling over my head here. So I just kind of stay put. Again, I have no concept of what it looks like outside. Will they be able to make their way to the front doors, move some debris out of the way, and come and get us? I am thinking, *Get to Chief Prunty!* Just pull the debris up, and get to him. And I am still thinking that we can work our way down the stairway.

Making Contact

But then I start getting my Mayday message out, and the first solid hit I get is Deputy Chief Tom Haring. He says: "Okay, Ladder 6, I got you. I have you recorded. I have exactly where you are; you're in the B stairway." So that was good. I said all right, they know where we are.

But then Battalion Chief John Salka gets on the radio, and he calls for me specifically. "This is Battalion 18 to Ladder 6. Where are you? We'll come to look for you." So I gave him the pinpoint location, and then my neighbor Chris Dabner of Rescue 3 radios me. Chief Sal Visconti contacts me. He is an old friend, and I feel really good that he is on the other side of the airwave. I also let him know what to my knowledge is our location, and it is all very comforting to know they are on to us.

Then I hear Chief Billy Blaich, who used to be the captain of Engine 9, which was the engine in our firehouse. His son is in Engine 9 right now, so there is a definite connection. The chief and I are friends, and he tells me that he can approximate exactly where we are, the exact location. He's such a squared-away guy, precise, a colonel in the Marine Corps Reserves.

He tells me, "I have everybody off duty from Ladder 6 and Ladder 11, and we're coming to get you." It is also good knowing not just anybody is coming to get me, but guys who have a personal stake for my safety.

There are a whole bunch of guys who are zeroing in on my transmissions because my transmissions are the only ones getting out.

I'm thinking, *Nobody in front of me was bleeding to death, and we were safe.* I feel as long as we are safe in the stairway we just have to figure out what's the best way to go. We don't want to make a move just to make a move. We want to make a move that we know is going to be productive, and is going to get us out of the situation. So we are evaluating everything. . . .

Survival Mode

We now go into this survival mode kind of thing. I don't want anybody to use their masks. I say, "We are breathing the dust, and it is irritating, but it is breathable. We are hearing on the radio that guys are coming, and they are asking to have hose stretched. We may have a fire to deal with in a little while. I don't know. So don't use your masks if you don't have to. Don't use your flashlights 'cause we may be here tonight."

There's a little bit of light, but not enough for us to realize that even in a collapse, we are in good shape relative to what could be. When I was roaming around the stairway before, I broke into the fourth floor. I found a toilet there, and there are eleven of us in this stairway. So it won't flush, but at least we can cover it up afterwards, and we won't be smelling human waste while we are trapped in this small area. The floor area is not more than fifteen by fifteen feet.

Matt Komoroski broke into the third floor, and they found some sprinkler pipes. They thought that down the road we can break into these pipes and maybe get some water.

We find an elevator shaft, and the door is warped a little

bit. I shine my flashlight down and I could see other floors below us. I say, "We have the lifesaving rope, and could rappel down the elevator shaft and get in the lower floors." But then I think, *There is no guarantee we could get in on the lower floor. And then how do we get back up?* So maybe that is not a good idea. That goes on the back burner for Day 2 or 3, if we get desperate. We all seem to be patient. We're looking, we're transmitting Mayday messages, trying to get a grasp of what our situation really is.

A Ray of Sunshine

And then, about three to three-and-a-half hours later, all of a sudden a ray of sunshine breaks through the smoke and the dust. Once we see that, I say, "Okay, guys, there is supposed to be 106 floors above us, but now I see sunshine. There is nothing above us."

Rich Picciotto says, "That's it, Jay, this is our way out, we're out of here."

I say, "Rich, it probably is."

It takes another twenty minutes, and it clears up enough again, and then off in the distance we see a fireman from Ladder 43, about one hundred feet away from us.

Rescue

Never until this moment did we realize that there was sky above us, that we were virtually at the top of the collapsed building. [In the end] we were able to pull ourselves out. Just seeing Ladder 43 was enough for us to realize that this was our way out. We decide that Rich Picciotto will go. We tie him off on the lifesaving rope, and we put a special rescue knot on it. I had Billy Butler tie off with a Munter Hitch, which acts like a seatbelt. It plays out fine, but if there is a sudden jolt it will lock off. I want that knot used because if Rich falls, we will be able to retrieve him.

Richie goes out, and it had to be about a hundred feet before he meets the guy from 43 Truck. Richie ties off his rope on a beam that is sticking up out there. We tie it off on our end, and now I start sending the guys out. [First to go is]

Mike Meldrum, who has been beaten up pretty bad. In the meantime, half of our people are out before 43 Truck gets this far in to the stairway.

The guys have to walk on a ledge to get out of the stairway, hold on to this rope, and drop down. There is a lot of sharp metal all around us, and it was good to have that rope up for stability. I'm glad we didn't leave it behind.

The firefighters from Ladder 43 started coming in, and I meet Lieutenant Glenn Rohan. To me he is the handsomest man I ever saw, and I tell him that when things settle down, I'm going to stop by with a box of canolis. I then give him a briefing, and tell him about Chief Prunty.

When I get out and onto a clear pile, I see that 7 World Trade Center and the Customs House have serious fire. Almost every window has fire. It is an amazing sight.

The Customs House is immediately adjacent to this area, and the Secret Service ammunition bunker is there. Just as I get out, that starts exploding. So there's smoke from that, and the smoke from 7 World Trade Center is now coming across this debris pile. And there are two large two-story-deep craters that we have to crawl down into and climb up out of, using ropes to pull ourselves up. It is an ordeal, and it takes us a half hour just to make that trek from the stairway to West Street. From there we have to go through the World Financial Center to get where the ambulances were. All in all there were fourteen of us in there, eleven of us, Lieutenant McGlynn, and two firefighters from Engine 39.

Now we're on the other side of the World Financial Center, and I keep saying, "Where's the command post, where's the command post?"

The guy says, "Don't worry about the command post. Go get treated, go to the ambulance."

A Touching Moment

I say, "No, there was a lot of guys coming for us." I know I have to check in. I don't want anybody getting hurt looking for me, especially when I'm out. So I make my way to the command post, and Peter Hayden and Jim DeDominico are standing on top of a fire truck in front of the fire so they can see across the debris. I get to the base of the truck and, naturally, there's hundreds of guys and all kinds of noise, and I yell up, "Chief Hayden, Chief Hayden!"

I finally get his attention, and it is a very touching moment for me, and I guess for him, because I love working for him, and he loves having me. We have a long relationship, very positive, and he looks down, and I can see him tearing up a little bit. He says, "Jay, it's good to see you."

I just hold up my hand, saying, "It's good to be here."

I think he says something like, "Well, now you're going to get promoted to battalion chief." I think that it will be good to be around for that.

Looking at the tremendous devastation before me, I cannot believe that we have survived it. It wasn't until later that I realized that if we didn't stop to help Josephine, we would have probably been in the lobby or just outside the building where everyone perished. Engine 28, who had gone past us, were running at top speed to get free of the collapse, and they just made it. And then, to think that all of these men I have talked about, Terry Hatton, Paddy Brown, Dave Weiss, Jerry Nevins, Faustino Apostol, Mike Warchola, and Richard Prunty, are gone—it is just too terrible to speak about.

Back to the Firehouse

I get some medical treatment, and they want to take me to a hospital. All I want to do is get back to the firehouse. I can't find any transportation. Our truck is completely flattened. On West Street I see a couple of sector cars parked with one patrolman there.

I grab him and say, "You have got to give me a ride."

He says, "Oh, man, I'm not supposed to leave here."

"Can you give me a ride at least halfway?"

"I'll give you a ride to Canal Street."

I say, "Well, that's something." So he drives me to Canal and he's all nervous—he's a young officer.

I get out, and I start walking. I get to Broadway and I see there's no traffic. I have worked this neighborhood for years and I've never seen Canal Street with no traffic. But there are a lot of pedestrians, and they begin following me like I'm the Pied Piper. I still have all my gear on, but I'm dirty—like Pig Pen in Charles Schulz's Peanuts cartoon, with a big cloud of dust [trailing behind] me. About thirty people are following, giving me water. Someone says, "Oh, my God, are you okay?" These are all Chinese people, and they usually keep to themselves.

I say, "I'm better than most."

"You're Alive"

Meantime, I am trying to get a word out to my wife, Judy, and I can't get through. I try one more time, on a cell that belongs to someone from Engine 9. I get a phone call out, and I am talking to Judy. She just keeps crying on the phone, repeating over and over, "You're alive, you're alive, you're alive."

And I just keep on saying, "I love you, I love you, I love you."

A Firefighter's Worst Nightmare

Dennis Smith

The firefighters and police officers who rushed into the twin towers of the World Trade Center after the terrorist attacks had no idea they were going to their deaths. The first tower collapsed without warning, killing thousands of people still inside. Those in the second tower who were aware of the first tower's collapse had a few minutes' warning and many were able to get out in time. Hundreds of lives were saved by the evacuation, but the list of dead or missing includes entire companies of firefighters, police officers, and other emergency personnel. Reports list 403 rescue personnel as killed or still missing.

Dennis Smith retired from the Fire Department of New York in 1981, but when he heard about the disaster, he put on his old FDNY clothes, grabbed his identification, and went to see how he could help. In the following essay, Smith describes what the area around the towers was like after the collapse. He thinks about his friends and colleagues who risked—and gave—their lives to save others. He believes their sacrifice will inspire others to go on with their lives.

The second tower has just collapsed. I am at ladder 16, and the firefighters have commandeered a crowded 67th Street cross-town bus. We go without stopping from Lexington Avenue to the staging center on Amsterdam. We don't talk much on the bus, and not a single passenger complains about missing his or her stop.

At Amsterdam we board another bus, and here the quiet is broken by a Lieutenant who says, "We'll see things today we shouldn't have to see and there will be things we might think we should attend to, but listen up, we'll do it together. We'll be together, and we'll all come back together boys." He opens a box of dust masks and gives two to each of us.

It is like approaching a beach as we walk down West Street, passing hundreds of waiting emergency vehicles. First there is a little concrete dust, like powdered soft sand, and then suddenly every step kicks up a cloud. There is paper debris everywhere, strewn between window casings, air conditioner grates, and large chunks of what had once been the tallest structures in the world.

We report to the command chief who is standing ankle deep in mud between the World Trade Center (WTC) and the World Financial Center. The original command chief, Peter Ganci, along with the physical command center are missing, now somewhere beneath these mountains of cracked concrete and bent steel of the second collapse.

Just before that collapse, a falling woman killed a firefighter and Father Judge was giving him the last rites. Bill Feehan, the First Deputy Commissioner, was standing next to them. And then the building came down.

Not Much to Do

Now several hundred firefighters are milling about. There is not much for us to do except pull hose from one location to another as a pumper and a ladder truck are repositioned. It is like the eye of a storm, eerily quiet, and so unlike the multiple alarm emergencies I am used to. No sirens. No helicopters. Just the sound of two hose lines, watering the six stories of the hotel on West Street that are still standing. The low cackle of the department radios fade into solemn air. The danger is now presented by the burning 47-storey building (WTC Building) before us, just to the North of the World Trade Center. The command chief has ordered the firefighters from that building, and we are now waiting for it to collapse.

I want to see the destruction from the Liberty Street side of the buildings, and I travel through the World Financial Center, the headquarters of American Express and Merrill Lynch. There has been a complete evacuation, and I am the only person in the building. It seems the building has been abandoned for fifty years, for there are several inches of dust on the floors. The large and beautiful atrium of the buildings is in ruins, the eastside wall completely demolished, and the glass canopy above broken through and hanging in large and threatening pieces.

Because of the pervasive gray dusting, I cannot read the street signs as I make my way to the other side. Many cars and trucks are overturned. From here I can see the gaping holes in the side of the Verizon Building. There is a lone fire company down a narrow street wetting down a smoldering pile. The mountains of debris in every direction are fifty and sixty feet high. I am still stunned by the wreckage, and it is only now that I begin to think of the human toll, of the silent thousands that are unseen before me in this utter ruin.

I am again on the West Street side, and the chiefs begin to push us back towards the Hudson. Number 7 is about to fall, and when it does, we all think to run for cover, into stores, behind ambulances, around a corner. But, it is an incredible thing to watch a 47-storey building fall. The regality of a high building is transformed in few seconds to mere rubble. And now, I think that this building has fallen on those we seek.

The Lost and Missing

No one wants to say a number. We know that entire companies are unaccounted for. The department's elite squads, Rescue 1, Rescue 2, Rescue 3, and Rescue 4 are not heard from. Just last week I talked with a group of Rescue 1 firefighters about the difficult and rigid prerequisites to get into the rescue companies—the endorsements from other company commanders and the tests of mechanical and engineering skills. I remember thinking then that these were truly unusual men, smart and thoughtful, the kind of men into whose arms I would put the lives of my children. I know the Captain of Rescue 1, Terry Hatten. He is married to the Mayor's assistant, Beth Patrone, and one of those universally loved and respected men in the job. I think about Terry, and about Paddy Brown. Paddy is one of a small cadre of the most decorated firefighters in the history of the department, and in the nineties he was on the front page of all newspapers when he lowered one of his men on a rope to pick up a victim in a Times Square fire. And I think of Brian Hickey, the Captain of Rescue 4, who just last month survived the blast of the Astoria fire that killed three firefighters including two of his own men. I remember the sadness in his eyes at the funerals. And, now. . . he was working with Rescue 3 today. And then there is Ray Downey, the Battalion Chief who led the FDNY collapse specialists to Oklahoma City, a solid and giving man.

I am pulling a heavy six-inch hose through the muck when I see Mike Carter, the Vice-president of the firefighters union, on the hose just before me. He's a good friend, and we barely say hello to each other. I see Kevin Gallagher, the union president, who is looking for his son who is unaccounted for. Someone calls to me. It is Jimmy Boyle, the retired president of the union, the man who gave us such great leadership in my time on the job. "I can't find Michael," he says. Michael Boyle, his son, was with Engine 33, and the whole company is missing. I can't say anything to Jimmy, but just throw my arms around him.

The immediate danger over, the army of construction workers, police officers, EMTs and firefighters begin to work. People who have never met begin working side by side as if they practiced for months. Cars are lifted, hoses and fire trucks moved, and the heavy equipment is brought in. As I watch the steelworkers they progress in my mind from admirable to heroic.

I don't have boots and I am wet to the knees. I will "take up" as we say, and go home. At the end of this horrific day I think of Shakespeare's line about evil living forever, and I realize how most of the good of everything I know about this world is interred beneath the rubble before me. It will be days before there is a final accounting, and I can only hope against hope for the people that I have mentioned. They have been friends of mine for many years. It was from their lives that New York's firefighters learned how to keep their chins up in danger, and how to get down on their knees when help is needed. It is because of them, and this terrible number of lost firefighters, whatever number that might be, that inspiration will be found to go on with our lives.

The last thing I see is Kevin Gallagher kissing another firefighter. It is his son.

Counting Bodies

Sandeep Jauhar

In the first hours of the attack, nearby hospitals were warned to be ready for thousands of wounded. Doctors, nurses, and emergency medical personnel rushed to the area to provide assistance. People flocked to hospitals to give blood. It soon became clear, however, that there would be very few injured who needed help. Rescuers searched in the rubble for days, hoping that they would find survivors buried in the wreckage. As the hours and days passed, hope dwindled and medical workers were pressed into other jobs.

Sandeep Jauhar, a new doctor, presented himself at Ground Zero the day after the attack hoping to be of some help. He was told to report to the makeshift morgue where doctors were needed to supervise the collection and cataloging of bodies and body parts. It was a job that he never dreamed he would be doing and one he found difficult to perform.

The morgue was inside Brooks Brothers [a clothing store]. I was standing at the open-air triage center at the corner of Church and Dey, right next to the rubble of the World Trade Center, when a policeman shouted that doctors were needed at the menswear emporium inside the 1 Liberty building. Bodies were piling up there, he said, and another makeshift morgue on the other side of the rubble had just closed down. I volunteered and set off down the debris-strewn road.

It was the day after the attack. The smoke and stench of burning plastic was even stronger than on Tuesday. The road was muddy, and because I was stupidly wearing clogs, the mud soaked my socks.

I arrived at the building. In the lobby, exhausted fire-fighters and their German shepherds were sitting on the floor amid broken glass. A soldier stood at the entrance to the store, where a crowd of policemen hovered. "No one is allowed in the morgue except doctors," he shouted.

The Morgue

I entered reluctantly through a dark curtain. Cadavers had always made me feel queasy in medical school. In anatomy lab, I had mostly watched as others dissected. In the near corner was a small group of doctors and nurses, and next to them was an empty plastic stretcher. Behind the group was a wooden table where a nurse and two medical students were sitting grim-faced, looking like some sort of macabre tribunal. Brooks Brothers shirts were neatly folded in cub-byholes in the wall. They were covered in grime, but you could still make out the reds and oranges and yellows. In the far corner, next to what looked like a blown-out door, was a pile of orange body bags, about 20 of them. Soldiers were standing guard. In the store's dressing room were stacks of unused body bags.

The group was discussing the protocol for how to handle the bodies. A young female doctor said that she didn't think anyone should sign any forms, lest someone think that we had certified the contents of the bags, which we were not qualified to do. That, she said, was up to the medical exam-iner. Someone asked whether a separate body bag was needed for each body part, but no one knew the answer. The leader of the group was a man in his 50's. I looked at his badge. It said "PGY-3." He was a third-year resident, which meant that I was probably the most experienced doctor in the room, a thought that deeply disturbed me. I just finished my internal medicine residency in June 2001.

At this point some National Guardsmen brought in a body bag and laid it on the stretcher. The female doctor unzipped it and inspected the contents. "Holy mother of God," she said, and she turned away. In the bag was a left leg and part of a pelvis, to which a penis was still attached. The leg itself hardly seemed injured, but the pelvic stump was beefy red and broken intestines were hanging out of it. A pants pocket was partially covering the pelvis and was emptied of change; this pocket was put in a separate bag. A policeman said that part of the victim's body had been brought in earlier, along with a cell phone.

That was good news. If the victim had the numbers of family members on his speed dial, he would be quickly identified. But identification wasn't my job. Processing was.

Cataloging Body Parts

After five minutes, the bag was zipped up. The older male doctor, who had been working there for hours, said he had to leave. The other doctor also said she had to get away for about an hour. "Are you a physician?" she asked me. "Yes," I replied. "Great," she said. "You can take over." Then she started giving me instructions on how to catalog the body parts. Basically, I had to call out the contents of each bag to a nurse, who would write them down on a form. That was it.

I was in a fog. I felt totally unequipped to do this kind of work. I recalled my friends who had done medical clerkships in Africa. They had told me of the terrible tragedies and the deep frustration of not having proper medical supplies. But we were not suffering from a lack of supplies. This was not third-world medicine. It was netherworld medicine, without rules.

Another body bag came in. This one had a spleen, some intestines, part of a liver. I was in charge, but I wasn't a pathologist. I was just improvising. After sifting through the bag's contents, I began to feel ill. I walked past some headless mannequins and out into the smoke-filled air.

Searching for Bodies

Paul Morgan

After the World Trade towers collapsed, firefighters, police officers, and other rescue workers began arriving in a steady stream, ready to do whatever was necessary to look for survivors and the dead. Search-and-rescue dogs and their handlers also heard the call and came from all over the United States to lend their services.

Paul Morgan and his golden retriever, Cody, arrived at Ground Zero the day after the attacks and immediately began their search for survivors and bodies. Unfortunately, they did not find any survivors, but Cody found three sets of remains in the first thirty minutes they were on the site. The work was difficult and exhausting but Morgan was grateful he and his dog were able to be of service.

M y buddy, Hal Wilson, and I went into the "pile" at the World Trade Center with our search dogs, Cody and Sue, at 11 A.M. on Wednesday, September 12th, 2001. You wouldn't believe the teamwork and the silence with hundreds of firefighters stumbling through the mess. . . .

On the way in through the rubble we walked past deserted restaurants with white and checkered table cloths, fully stacked bars, wine on tables and menus in hallways which had survived the blast. Then the realization hit us head on as we entered a court yard and we saw the "pile" of debris several stories high.

We linked up with four state police K-9 teams which were the dirtiest, filthiest men and dogs we had ever seen.

They were covered with gray dust and mud. All of the troopers had that thousand meter stare which all combat veterans have after they have been on the line too long.

The troopers and their dirty dogs were being pulled out as Hal and I were deployed with Cody and Sue on to the "pile" stacked several stories high with fire rigs, police cars, twisted I beams, shards of glass, aluminum, wood and chunks of metal and concrete sticking out of the ground. The metal rods I stumbled through reminded me of punji stakes [a type of booby trap] in Vietnam.

Three Bodies in Thirty Minutes

The fire lieutenant in charge led Hal and I and our dogs to a fire rig which has been a hose truck. It was gray, completely burned out. . .no seats, dash, steering wheel. . .nothing. "Get down there, please, and tell me if you can detect anybody in there!" the officer requested. Cody and I climbed down ten feet and I called into the truck, "If you can hear me, say ONE, if you can hear me, say TWO, if you can hear me, say THREE!" There was no response. Then I repeated myself and said, "If you can hear me, but can't talk, bang the wall with your foot ONCE . . . TWICE . . . THREE TIMES!" Still no response. Cody, my golden retriever, began scratching and I told the fire fighters above me, "We have a body down here!"

They pulled Cody and me out of the pit and began cutting the truck open with an electric saw. Several minutes later I heard the fire fighters below call out, "Body Bag!"

As an orange plastic roll was passed down the line into the pit next to the burned out rig, another officer asked me, "How good is your dog?" We were standing on a hose line and Cody was scratching again. I didn't have to answer the officer when Cody's paws suddenly were covered with blood. "Body Bag!" was heard again and another roll of orange plastic was passed down the line.

The remains of the first fire fighter were carefully lifted to the surface in a basket and eight of his brothers carried the remains to the morgue truck. Soon the second fire fighter's remains Cody had discovered were placed into another body bag and we were asked to step aside as another crew removed them.

Another officer grabbed my arm and directed me to a concrete slab which had been a wall the day before. Under the slab was another fire rig. "Can you get down there and tell us if. . . ." He didn't have to finish the request. A hole had been punched into the wall of debris below the slab. "What's down there?" somebody asked.

Cody and I climbed down into this pit and I stuck my nose into the hole, smelling gas. Then Cody passed by me digging into the debris under the slab. We smelled burnt flesh again and I signalled the officer behind me. "Body Bag!" was heard again.

I couldn't believe Cody had discovered three sets of remains in thirty minutes. It was more than I had ever expected from that dog.

As I tried to get out from under the slab and clear the way for another crew to remove remains, I found myself in a great deal of trouble. I was wedged into a pit and couldn't move. It was like being under a staircase in a dark basement and there was no way to get out.

Cody was still in front of me however and in a dash for his safety, gasping for air, he jumped over my left shoulder and turned me around. I crawled toward the light and was lifted to the surface by a squad of fire fighters which began to dismantle the slab under which we were trapped.

Exhausted and Hurting

I was exhausted this time so Cody and I returned to the top of the "pile" watching a body bag with remains being removed from the scene every twenty minutes or so.

Soon a wind picked up and we began dodging shrapnel flying off buildings about the pile. I thought I had seen it all in two years of Vietnam combat. I hadn't!

I couldn't find my helmet which was buried in my back pack under three days of rations I had loaded for Cody. "Helmets!" was the order so I stumbled away to the relative safety of another structure . . . one which collapsed later in the day . . . where two nurses gave us water and another provided us a cup of orange juice.

Then I got rattled, starting to look for my partner, Hal, and his dog. He was right behind me . . . and so was Sue . . . "Hey Marine . . . let's get the hell out of here!" I shouted. "Yes, sir!" he responded and we followed a crew of fire fighters carrying remains from the "pile" through the building with the bar and restaurants out to the morgue truck.

We were exhausted and hurting. Cody was sneezing and coughing so we headed for the Suffolk County SPCA van. But before we left the scene, Hal procured a metal tray from a garbage pile and we gave our dogs all the water we had . . . and as we did . . . a squad of fire fighters behind us poured out all their water into the tray for the dogs. Nobody said a word.

After the dogs were checked out by volunteer vets and vet techs at the Suffolk County SPCA, had their noses and eyes washed, paws cleaned and received shots, we were ordered to rest for an hour at Stuyvesant High School. We followed orders.

About 4 P.M. we started home, walking towards Penn Station on 34th Street. Sue was close to heat exhaustion and Cody was having a hard time breathing. Then we spotted a Franciscan priest who blessed the animals, Hal and me. We felt better and started on our way again. Cody stopped in his tracks on 23rd Street and 6th Avenue, unable to walk any longer.

We watered both dogs, taking a break on a sidewalk, leaning against an office building. Passersby said "Thanks!" and after a few minutes we were on our way again.

When we arrived at Penn Station, twenty minutes before our train was due to depart for Long Island, more people said, "Thanks!", providing us food, water and a couple of beers. On the train ride home Cody slept under my feet with his back to the a/c.

A Priest at Ground Zero

James Martin

Firefighters, police officers, and medical personnel were not the only ones working at Ground Zero. Religious leaders of all faiths also converged on the World Trade Center site to offer hope, comfort, support, and encouragement to the workers. James Martin, a Catholic priest and associate editor of *America* magazine, wanted desperately to be able to help somehow. He visited the World Trade Center to offer his help, only to discover that many other members of the clergy had preceded him. Then, in fear of what the answer might be, Martin asked if priests were needed at Ground Zero, and to his chagrin, he was quickly whisked to the site. There, Martin talked to the rescue workers and construction and military personnel about what they had seen, how they felt, and what they were thinking. He was in awe of their dedication to their job and realized that they were the epitome of love for their fellow man. The experience so moved him that when he left, he was temporarily disoriented, a humbling experience for a New Yorker who always knew where he was going.

Two days after the terrorist attack on the World Trade Center, I made my way to one of the emergency trauma centers in Manhattan. It had been hastily set up in a cavernous sports facility called Chelsea Piers, on the Hudson River.

Wanting to Help

I had been there earlier, on the evening of Sept. 11, still stunned from the day's events like many New Yorkers, and, also like many New Yorkers, wanting desperately to do something. But on that surreal and awful night, I simply waited with dozens of doctors, nurses, police officers, firefighters and volunteers for what officials expected would be hundreds of survivors. I ran into three young Franciscan friars, who were planning to spend the night there. They were full of energy and devotion. But though we wanted to help, after a few hours the stunning reality dawned: there would not be many survivors to attend to.

When I return to Chelsea Piers two days later to offer assistance, I discover that I have already been preceded by scores of members of the clergy. "Another priest," says one harried, sweating volunteer as I enter. "Go upstairs and ask for Ellen." Ellen tells me that she already has plenty of priests, ministers and rabbis. I wander downstairs, trying to think about where I might be able to help most. The day before I had spent at a center set up by a local Catholic hospital, where family members painfully searched dog-eared sheets of paper that listed the names of survivors. But at that hospital too there was a surfeit of help: there are so many mental-health care professionals in Manhattan.

Outside, surrounded by ambulances, U.S. Army vehicles, police cars, fire engines and dump trucks, I ask a police sergeant a question upon which I had reflected not at all. But it seems the right thing to ask: Do you think they might be able to use a priest downtown?

He knows where I mean. And I am terrified he will say yes.

Of course, he says yes. Almost instantly a police car materializes to bring me to the site of the former World Trade Center. One of my spiritual directors used to say that sometimes if God wants you to do something, he removes all roadblocks, and I feel this intensely as we sail downtown. I ask, he answers, we go.

My own fear increases with every southerly block. With me in the back seat is a well-dressed psychiatrist. "Have you dealt with trauma victims?" he asks, as we speed through the streets. No, I say; please give me some advice. He does.

The sights of the first few minutes of the drive are familiar, comforting: the river on the right, the Manhattan skyline on the left. We make a lefthand turn, and there are fewer and fewer people walking on the street. When we stop briefly at an intersection, crowds of people surround the car, cheering and clapping, waving flags. My window is open, and a hand is thrust in, offering muffins, donuts, bottled water. We turn again, and presently there are many parked cars covered with fine soot. Our car passes the line that cordons off the press from the rescue area; I see cameras, reporters, news vans. And then we make another turn: here are cars crushed by falling debris, papers floating in the breeze, and more and more pale grey ash. We continue on and I catch sight of a burned, twisted building. The psychiatrist gets out of the car, wishes me well and sprints away.

A Repellent Sight

The car turns once again, and I see the sight familiar from repeated viewings on television: the horrible remains of the Trade Center, issuing forth a brown, acrid smoke that chokes one and brings tears to the eyes. It is repellent. I feel the urge at once to vomit and to weep.

A U.S. Army soldier walks over and greets me, providing me with a sort of friendly escort. Ashamed that I cannot tear my gaze from the site of the embrowned buildings only a few yards away, I make an effort to ask after the soldier's welfare. But, instead, he ministers to me. "That's O.K., Father," he says. "Everybody stares when they see it. It's hard to see, isn't it?" He hands me a face mask, which I notice everyone is wearing, to protect against the smoke and dust.

"Okay, Father," he says and points. "Just over there, that's where everyone is; it's the morgue." The temporary morgue is a formerly tony office building that, though I know the area well, I am now totally unable to recognize.

Hell and Grace

The streets surrounding the morgue are covered by two inches of soot. More paper blows around; I notice an office memo with its edges charred brown. Twisted girders covered with grime must be stepped over. All I can think of is a banality. But, though banal, it is true: this is like hell—full of immense sadness and terror and pathos.

And yet, here is grace. There are hundreds of rescue workers: firefighters and police officers and army personnel and construction workers and truck drivers and counselors and doctors and nurses. Almost all are in motion. They are purposeful, efficient, hard-working.

Some of the the firefighters and police officers sit by a staging area near the doorway of the temporary morgue, resting. Though most are New Yorkers, a surprising number are not, having traveled great distances (from Massachusetts, says one; from Florida, says another) to help. We talk about what they have seen, how they feel, what they think. In the midst of this hell, they are inspiring to speak with, and say simple things, made profound to me by their situation: "Just doing my job, Father." "One day at a time." "Doing the best I can, Father." I cannot resist the urge to tell them what great work they are doing.

Suddenly I realize that I am standing beside grace. Here are men and women, some of whom tell me "I lost a buddy in there," who are going about their business—a business that includes the possibility of dying. "Greater love has no person," said Jesus, "than the one who lays down his life for another." And this is what that looks like. Here it is.

As I think this, four men carry a small orange bag past us holding the remains of a victim of the attack. I am afraid of what I might see, so I do not look.

Next to the building, three African-American N.Y.P.D. officers sit on salvaged office chairs in front of cardboard boxes that are stacked perhaps six feet high. We talk about their work here. All are New Yorkers, who say how disorienting it is to consider downtown without the World Trade

Center. We talk about friends we know who were at or near the Trade Center at the time.

A Familiar Story

One of my friends, I tell them, who worked at a nearby building, emerged from his subway station at 9:00 a.m. on Tuesday, as crowds of people raced by. "What happened?" he asks someone. "A plane hit the World Trade Center!" He goes to his office anyway; he thinks it must have been a small plane that hit. No need to worry.

Once at his desk, he looks out the window and sees the appalling sight of the Trade Center wreathed in smoke. When he tells me the story, he pauses, and says what many New Yorkers say, "I couldn't believe it. I couldn't understand it." Now he rushes to the stairwells with co-workers, and begins racing down 18 floors. Once outside, a police officer shouts at him. "Run! Run! Run!" As he runs, dazed, someone cries out, "It's collapsing!" He tells me he thinks to himself: don't be surprised if you die.

The police officers nod. They know many similar stories, and, of course, far worse ones. It is hard to take it all in, one says. They talk more about their experiences and say they are worried that it will get worse once the recovery of the bodies begins. "Here are the bags," says one, gesturing behind him, and it is suddenly clear what is in that tall pile of boxes.

When I feel that I have talked with as many people as I can (at least those who are not busy with their work), I leave. One police sergeant tells me the way out: walk up this path, he says. As I do, streams of fire companies pass me, and almost everyone greets me. "Hello, Father." They touch the brim of their helmets. They shake my hand as I leave and they move in toward the wreckage.

A Different World

Leaving is stranger than coming. All I have to do is walk north. The rubble eventually recedes, so there is nothing to step over; the soot becomes less distinct and the pavements are cleaner; the smoke clears and I remove my mask; there are more and more pedestrians. And then I am back in New York on a sunny fall day: people in Greenwich Village sit in outdoor cafes; women in tank tops jog by; taxis race past. I remember reading about soldiers in World War I who would fight in the trenches in France during the day and then, granted a day's leave, would be in the theaters of London in the evening. Is this what it is like for the rescue workers? A subway entrance presents itself. A policeman sees me and walks over. I suddenly realize I must look strange: in clerics, sweating, covered in grey soot, a face mask dangling from my neck. "What subway do you want?" I am astonished to find out that I am so disoriented that I cannot tell him, but can only say that I want to go uptown. I feel foolish—a New Yorker takes pride in knowing where he's going. "Were you down there?" he asks. I nod and he brings me downstairs, past the ticket counter, and motions for the subway attendant to open up the gate, to allow me in for a free ride, a last gesture of kindness and solidarity in a city overwhelmed by grief but united in overwhelming charity.

A Night at Ground Zero

Erin Bertocci

People everywhere were horrified by the spectacle of the
burning twin towers and their subsequent collapse. They felt
the urgent need to do something to help. Erin Bertocci's
chance to help came when she heard that the firefighters
needed some coffee. She and her roommate collected cans of
coffee, hot pizzas, and jugs of water, and brought them down
to the staging area near the World Trade Center. Once there,
she found work organizing all the supplies that had been
donated for the rescue workers. Bertocci describes the reactions the workers had when she occasionally ran out of some
necessary supply; instead of becoming angry or upset, she
was amazed that they still thanked her for her help. Their
work and dedication was inspiring.

A fter hearing the reports on television that no one could
get down to the epicenter of this tragedy, I basically
had reserved a spot on the couch for my third night in a row
of watching and waiting, wishing I could "do more."

Randomly, one reporter invited some teenager on the air
to say what supplies were needed down at the scene, and the
boy said, "The firefighters need coffee." So I looked at my
friend who was similarly camped on the couch next to me,
and we both said, "We can get coffee."

One can of coffee became four cans . . . and three pizza
pies and gallon jugs of water, which we shepherded into a

taxi to head down to Chelsea Piers, where this boy said coffee was needed. Chelsea Piers are huge—there's an ice skating rink, golf practice area, community gyms. . . . I wasn't sure where to stop, but when we saw some firefighters standing among some boxes, we thought they might like some pizza. It turns out that this area was a loading area for community stores to donate goods—supplies of paper towels, cloth towels, immense packs of bottled water, vast quantities of Quaker Chewy Granola Bars. Individuals also brought supplies—a six-pack of soda, clothing like T-shirts and pants for the firefighters, boxer shorts. One young boy came over with his parents, struggling under the weight of a gallon cranberry juice bottle, label half peeled off, which he proudly said he had filled with water for the "policemen who fight fires."

Without being told what to do, everyone fell into line, the "pass the bucket" variety in which you grab from your right and pass to your left, to get everything off the trucks and into piles on the pier. One by one, NYC Police Department Harbor Patrol boats would drive up to the pier to be loaded with supplies to be brought down to the firemen and policemen working at the site. With three big tins of heated ziti in hand, I boarded the boat . . . and only when I was handed a filtered mask did I fully realize where I was headed.

A Different World

The trip down the Hudson River was short . . . and it was a beautiful, warm night. Any other night it would have been gorgeous. Any other night the New York City skyline wouldn't have had a giant cloud of white smoke billowing up into darkness. The air quality definitely worsened as we approached the dock. The last time I had been on that exact dock was a few years ago when my project threw a dinner cruise for a client. This could not possibly have been more different from that evening, when the windows glistened, and the flags along the harbor flapped wildly in the wind. Now, the flags were still, at half-mast. The buildings were covered in white-gray dust. Paperwork of those who used to work so far above lay strewn all over the pier. Whole chunks of buildings near the towers were peeled out from their place, sides of a building looked like a banana peel of window frames and twisted metal. The World Financial Center glass atrium, the Winter Garden, was a ghostly metal frame

Lending a Helping Hand

People were overwhelmed by the tragedy of the attacks against the World Trade Center and wanted to do whatever they could to help. However, only a small number of people—firefighters, police, medical personnel, clergy, and reserve troops—were permitted to enter the site; ordinary civilians were kept blocks away behind police barricades. Yet that did not stop people from coming to Ground Zero to offer whatever help and support they could. Craig Childs, author of The Secret Knowledge of Water, *was in New York when the World Trade Center was attacked. He recorded his observations of being near Ground Zero for National Public Radio.*

In the night, I walked along the Hudson River where maybe a hundred people had gathered. Smoke poured between the buildings around us from nearby debris. Wearing bandanas and dust masks, we applauded the streams of emergency vehicles leaving ground zero, we shouted out thanks and the vehicles kept coming—ambulances, troop trucks full of dusty rescuers, semi trucks loaded with huge tangles of metal and stairways and window glass.

I reached out and high-fived a paramedic sticking her arm from the ambulance window. The workers stared at us in disbelief. Expressions of confused joy began to appear on their faces, as they honked and flashed their lights. In the other lane, a steady rush of replacement vehicles, sirens blaring, headed downtown.

When I finally walked away into the next street, faint with smoke, my hands hurt from all the clapping. If I couldn't lift wreckage and search for survivors, at least my hands were sore from supporting those who could.

Craig Childs, National Public Radio, September 18, 2001.

with some window panes still intact—but the only lights reflected on the few remaining windows came not from the internal lights, but the eerie refraction from the bright work lights being used at the site. With dust on everything, with buildings cut and windows blown out, it looked very much like a movie set—the glass atrium like the model for the *Millennium Falcon* from *Star Wars,* and the rest like a set that was painted in the same matte colors without differentiation. Almost like a science fiction cartoon picture.

We took the supplies off the boat and brought them to the principal loading area by the pier. Since we expected rain, everything had been moved under the building ledges where restaurant outdoor cafés once stood. Piles of clothing and towels, medical supplies, work supplies like shovels and pick axes, and food lay arranged in their proper area . . . and from there as needed would be taken from their large storage areas to the "up front" area. Clutching pans of pasta, I sloshed through the mud puddles and navigated around the fire hoses that lay all over the ground, through what was once the World Financial Center complex. Volunteers had written messages in the dust that covered windows: "Let's Show the World," "America Stand Strong" and "Thank You." I walked through the building and emerged on the plaza side, facing what was once the World Trade Center towers. The mass of twisted steel, heaps of concrete and huge polished metal sidings of what was once the WTC . . . it's just like what's on television, but it's huge. Firemen were climbing all over these huge piles, covering the mounds of rubble, passing buckets of rubble one-by-one. It was unreal. The sheer volume of volunteers milling around was so impressive—and the horribly immense pile of material to be cleared was unimaginable. Just when you might have thought you were at a construction site, or a junkyard, you'd find a shoe. Just laying there.

A Humbling Experience

After passing out food briefly, I spent the next nine hours reorganizing their supplies inside what was once One Financial Center. The escalators were still, and dirt was everywhere, but the roof was solid . . . and would provide needed protection from the expected rain. I was humbled by the police and firefighters who were volunteering. When I asked one fireman if he wanted to lie down to rest, he pointed at a picture of his wife and daughter, which was taped to his arm. "Every time I get tired, I think of them, and I have the energy I need." A number of policemen there were "off-duty"—the force didn't want them to risk injury, so they aren't allowed to work there while on the job. On their off hours, however, they can do as they like . . . and after working twelve- to sixteen-hour shifts, they're back at Ground Zero, ready to help. One policeman has a compromise with his terrified wife that he'll call her every hour to tell her that he's okay.

The rain came pounding down, and still they stayed out there. We ran out of rain gear, and I hated to tell them we didn't have anything to keep them dry. We even ran out of garbage bags for a while from which they had been fashioning slickers. Rather than get all huffy or mad, they simply shrugged and said, "That's okay, thanks for your help." We ran out of long-sleeve shirts for a while, and though they must have been freezing, when I gave them the news they said, "Okay, thank you for looking." I don't know any of their names, because they all referred to each other as "Brother." They helped me to carry my carts of clothing over the fire hoses and were incredibly polite. They made sure I wasn't cold and continually asked me if I had eaten anything. I couldn't believe with everything they were doing, they took the time to check on me.

I had no idea what kind of wonderful, caring people we have protecting our city. These people will not give up. They just keep going out there. They nap for a few minutes, and then they're right back on the pile. It was a privilege to help out, even just for a little while, to "do more." They were there when I arrived in the evening and they remained after I left in the morning . . . they will not leave . . . and they're simply remarkable. My heart goes out to them.

Chapter 3

The Western World's Response

Chapter Preface

A mericans and others around the world were glued to their television sets in the first hours and days after the attacks of September 11, 2001. They watched in shock, disbelief, fear, sadness, and anger as television networks replayed the footage of the planes crashing into the towers and the towers' subsequent collapse. Many could not fully comprehend the reality of the situation, and remarked that it seemed as if they were watching a movie. For many New Yorkers, the twin towers had dominated their lives every day, and they were stunned by the hole their absence made in the skyline.

When the terrorists attacked the World Trade Center towers, they destroyed not only a symbol of America—one that awed all those who saw them towering 110 stories into the sky—but Americans' feelings of power, privilege, and confidence. After the attacks, Americans suddenly felt vulnerable, weak, and afraid, as well as outraged and full of grief for the thousands who were wounded and killed.

Much of the world shared their feelings of anger and mourning, and foreign displays of solidarity were comforting to shell-shocked Americans. Americans abroad reported that strangers offered their condolences. American embassies from London to Moscow were deluged with bouquets of flowers, sympathy cards, and lit candles. For the first time in history, the American anthem was played during the changing of the guards at Buckingham Palace in London. And leaders from around the world called President George W. Bush at the White House to express their horror over the attacks and sorrow over the deaths and destruction.

Bush and New York City mayor Rudy Giuliani emerged from the rubble of their respective cities and their presence reassured the country and New York that the United States would survive and recover. Both men appeared at Ground Zero, the site where the World Trade Center towers once stood, and breathed the dust-laden air and experienced the anguish of the rescuers as they searched for survivors. The leaders took charge—Bush of the nation, Giuliani of his city—and instilled confidence by putting protective measures into place and hailing the heroic efforts of everyone involved in the crisis.

Another leader who stands out for his leadership is Tony Blair, Great Britain's prime minister. Within hours of the attack, Blair was promising that England would stand shoulder to shoulder with the United States in fighting the war against terrorism. His support was instrumental in helping Bush line up an international coalition to fight Osama bin Laden, the suspected mastermind of the September 11 attacks, and his al-Qaeda terrorist network.

America Will Withstand This Attack

George W. Bush

George W. Bush, the forty-third president of the United States, was visiting an elementary school in Florida when the World Trade Center and the Pentagon were attacked by terrorists. Shortly after he returned to the White House, Bush gave a televised speech, excerpted below, in which he consoles Americans and reassures them that the United States will overcome these attacks.

Today, our fellow citizens, our way of life, our very freedom came under attack in a series of deliberate and deadly terrorist acts. The victims were in airplanes, or in their offices; secretaries, businessmen and women, military and federal workers; moms and dads, friends and neighbors. Thousands of lives were suddenly ended by evil, despicable acts of terror.

Our Country Is Strong

The pictures of airplanes flying into buildings, fires burning, huge structures collapsing, have filled us with disbelief, terrible sadness, and a quiet, unyielding anger. These acts of mass murder were intended to frighten our nation into chaos and retreat. But they have failed; our country is strong.

A great people has been moved to defend a great nation.

From George W. Bush's address to the nation, September 11, 2001.

Terrorist attacks can shake the foundations of our biggest buildings, but they cannot touch the foundation of America. These acts shattered steel, but they cannot dent the steel of American resolve.

America was targeted for attack because we're the brightest beacon for freedom and opportunity in the world. And no one will keep that light from shining.

Today, our nation saw evil, the very worst of human nature. And we responded with the best of America—with the daring of our rescue workers, with the caring for strangers and neighbors who came to give blood and help in any way they could.

Immediately following the first attack, I implemented our government's emergency response plans. Our military is powerful, and it's prepared. Our emergency teams are working in New York City and Washington, D.C. to help with local rescue efforts.

Open for Business

Our first priority is to get help to those who have been injured, and to take every precaution to protect our citizens at home and around the world from further attacks.

The functions of our government continue without interruption. Federal agencies in Washington which had to be evacuated today are reopening for essential personnel tonight, and will be open for business tomorrow. Our financial institutions remain strong, and the American economy will be open for business, as well.

The search is underway for those who are behind these evil acts. I've directed the full resources of our intelligence and law enforcement communities to find those responsible and to bring them to justice. We will make no distinction between the terrorists who committed these acts and those who harbor them.

I appreciate so very much the members of Congress who have joined me in strongly condemning these attacks. And on behalf of the American people, I thank the many world leaders who have called to offer their condolences and assistance.

America and our friends and allies join with all those who want peace and security in the world, and we stand together to win the war against terrorism. Tonight, I ask for your prayers for all those who grieve, for the children whose worlds have been shattered, for all whose sense of safety and security has been threatened. And I pray they will be comforted by a power greater than any of us, spoken through the ages in Psalm 23: "Even though I walk through the valley of the shadow of death, I fear no evil, for You are with me."

This is a day when all Americans from every walk of life unite in our resolve for justice and peace. America has stood down enemies before, and we will do so this time. None of us will ever forget this day. Yet, we go forward to defend freedom and all that is good and just in our world.

The World Must Unite Against Terrorists

Tony Blair

> For most of its young history, the United States has had a
> close bond with England. The two countries have been allies
> in numerous conflicts and wars and have supported each
> other in other ways as well. The statement below is an excerpt
> of a speech given by Tony Blair, the prime minister of Great
> Britain, to the House of Commons a few days after the terror-
> ist attacks on the World Trade Center. Blair asserts that these
> attacks were not just on the United States but on democracy
> itself. The terrorists' goal is to frighten the United States and
> other democratic societies into abandoning or changing their
> beliefs, values, and ideals. Therefore, he argues it is impera-
> tive that the world stand together in the war against terrorism
> and those who support it.

Mr Speaker, I am grateful that you agreed to the recall
of Parliament to debate the hideous and foul events in
New York, Washington and Pennsylvania that took place on
Tuesday 11 September, 2001.

I thought it particularly important in view of the fact that
these attacks were not just attacks upon people and buildings; nor even merely upon the USA; these were attacks on
the basic democratic values in which we all believe so pas-
sionately and on the civilised world. It is therefore right that

Excerpted from Tony Blair's statement to the House of Commons, September 14, 2001.

Parliament, the fount of our own democracy, makes its democratic voice heard.

There will be different shades of opinion heard today. That again is as it should be.

But let us unite in agreeing this: what happened in the United States on Tuesday was an act of wickedness for which there can never be justification. Whatever the cause, whatever the perversion of religious feeling, whatever the political belief, to inflict such terror on the world; to take the lives of so many innocent and defenceless men, women, and children, can never ever be justified.

Let us unite too, with the vast majority of decent people throughout the world, in sending our condolences to the government and the people of America. They are our friends and allies. We the British are a people that stand by our friends in time of need, trial and tragedy, and we do so without hesitation now.

The Attacks

The events are now sickeningly familiar to us. Starting at 08.45 US time, two hijacked planes were flown straight into the twin towers of the World Trade Centre in New York. Shortly afterwards at 09.43, another hijacked plane was flown into the Pentagon in Washington.

At 10.05 the first tower collapsed; at 10.28 the second; later another building at the World Trade Center. The heart of New York's financial district was devastated, carnage, death and injury everywhere.

Around 10.30 we heard reports that a fourth hijacked aircraft had crashed south of Pittsburgh.

I would like on behalf of the British people to express our admiration for the selfless bravery of the New York and American emergency services, many of whom lost their lives.

As we speak, the total death toll is still unclear, but it amounts to several thousands.

Because the World Trade Center was the home of many big financial firms, and because many of their employees are British, whoever committed these acts of terrorism will have murdered at least a hundred British citizens, maybe many more. Murder of British people in New York is no different in nature from their murder in the heart of Britain itself. In the most direct sense, therefore, we have not just an interest but an obligation to bring those responsible to account.

An Apalling Death Toll

To underline the scale of the loss we are talking about we can think back to some of the appalling tragedies this House has spoken of in the recent past. We can recall the grief aroused by the [1988] tragedy at Lockerbie, [Scotland] in which 270 people were killed, 44 of them British [when Pan Am flight 103 exploded in midair]. In Omagh [in Northern Ireland in 1998,] the last terrorist incident to lead to a recall of Parliament, 29 people lost their lives. Each life lost a tragedy. Each one of these events a nightmare for our country. But the death toll we are confronting here is of a different order.

In the [1982] Falklands War 255 British Service men perished. During the [1992] Gulf War we lost 47.

In this case, we are talking here about a tragedy of epoch-making proportions. . . .

Our Priorities

There are three things we must now take forward urgently.

First, we must bring to justice those responsible. Rightly, President George W. Bush and the US Government have proceeded with care. They did not lash out. They did not strike first and think afterwards. Their very deliberation is a measure of the seriousness of their intent.

They, together with allies, will want to identify, with care, those responsible. This is a judgement that must and will be based on hard evidence.

Once that judgement is made, the appropriate action can be taken. It will be determined, it will take time, it will continue over time until this menace is properly dealt with and its machinery of terror destroyed.

But one thing should be very clear. By their acts, these

terrorists and those behind them have made themselves the enemies of the civilised world.

The objective will be to bring to account those who have organised, aided, abetted and incited this act of infamy; and those that harbour or help them have a choice: either to cease their protection of our enemies; or be treated as an enemy themselves.

Secondly, this is a moment when every difference between nations, every divergence of interest, every irritant in our relations, are put to one side in one common endeavour. The world should stand together against this outrage.

NATO has already, for the first time since it was founded in 1949, invoked Article 5 and determined that this attack in America will be considered as an attack against the Alliance as a whole.

The UN Security Council on Wednesday passed a resolution which set out its readiness to take all necessary steps to combat terrorism.

From Russia, China, the EU, from Arab states, from Asia and the Americas, from every continent of the world has come united condemnation. This solidarity should be maintained and translated into support for action.

We do not yet know the exact origin of this evil. But, if, as appears likely, it is so-called Islamic fundamentalists, we know they do not speak or act for the vast majority of decent law-abiding Muslims throughout the world. I say to our Arab and Muslim friends: neither you nor Islam is responsible for this; on the contrary, we know you share our shock at this terrorism; and we ask you as friends to make common cause with us in defeating this barbarism that is totally foreign to the true spirit and teachings of Islam.

And I would add that, now more than ever, we have reason not to let the Middle East Peace Process slip still further but if at all possible to reinvigorate it and move it forward.

Fighting Terrorism

Thirdly, whatever the nature of the immediate response to these terrible events in America, we need to re-think dramatically the scale and nature of the action the world takes to combat terrorism.

We know a good deal about many of these terror groups. But as a world we have not been effective at dealing with them.

And of course it is difficult. We are democratic. They are not. We have respect for human life. They do not. We hold essentially liberal values. They do not. As we look into these issues it is important that we never lose sight of our basic values. But we have to understand the nature of the enemy and act accordingly.

Civil liberties are a vital part of our country, and of our world. But the most basic liberty of all is the right of the ordinary citizen to go about their business free from fear or terror. That liberty has been denied, in the cruellest way imaginable, to the passengers aboard the hijacked planes, to those who perished in the trade towers and the Pentagon, to the hundreds of rescue workers killed as they tried to help.

So we need to look once more: nationally and internationally at extradition laws, and the mechanisms for international justice; at how these terrorist groups are financed and their money laundered: and the links between terror and crime and we need to frame a response that will work, and hold internationally.

For this form of terror knows no mercy; no pity, and it knows no boundaries.

We Must Act

And let us make this reflection. A week ago, anyone suggesting terrorists would kill thousands of innocent people in downtown New York would have been dismissed as alarmist. It happened. We know that these groups are fanatics, capable of killing without discrimination. The limits on the numbers they kill and their methods of killing are not governed by morality. The limits are only practical or technical. We know, that they would, if they could, go further and use chemical or biological or even nuclear weapons of mass destruction. We know, also, that there are groups or people, occasionally states, who trade the technology and capability for such weapons.

It is time this trade was exposed, disrupted, and stamped out. We have been warned by the events of 11 September. We should act on the warning.

So there is a great deal to do and many details to be filled in, much careful work to be undertaken over the coming days, weeks and months.

We need to mourn the dead; and then act to protect the living.

Terrorism has taken on a new and frightening aspect.

The people perpetrating it wear the ultimate badge of the fanatic: they are prepared to commit suicide in pursuit of their beliefs.

Our beliefs are the very opposite of the fanatics. We believe in reason, democracy and tolerance.

These beliefs are the foundation of our civilised world. They are enduring, they have served us well and as history has shown we have been prepared to fight, when necessary to defend them. But the fanatics should know: we hold these beliefs every bit as strongly as they hold theirs.

Now is the time to show it.

Americans Are Strong and Resilient

Rudy Giuliani

Although the Pentagon in Washington, D.C., was also attacked by the terrorists on September 11, New York City and its residents bore the brunt of the attacks. Thousands of New Yorkers were killed and the twin towers of the World Trade Center, the very symbol of New York for three decades, were nothing more than rubble.

New York City mayor Rudy Giuliani immediately stepped forward and was a strong leader for his city. He often appeared at Ground Zero, the site where the towers once stood. At a citywide prayer service held at Yankee Stadium shortly after the attacks, he offered words of comfort. In his prayer, excerpted below, Giuliani praises all the victims of the attacks, especially the rescuers who died while trying to save others. He also tells the story of a small chapel near the towers that stood undamaged while modern buildings around it were destroyed. That chapel, he concludes, is like New Yorkers and Americans—resilient and strong, able to stand tall while others fall in the face of adversity.

On September 11th, New York City suffered the darkest day in our history. It is now up to us to make this our finest hour.

Today we come together in the Capital of the World, as a united City. We're accompanied by religious leaders of every faith, to offer a prayer for the families of those who

From Rudy Giuliani's speech at the citywide prayer service at Yankee Stadium, September 23, 2001.

have been lost . . . to offer a prayer for our City . . . and to offer a prayer for America.

The proud Twin Towers that once crowned our famous skyline no longer stand. But our skyline will rise again. In the words of President George W. Bush, "we will rebuild New York City."

To those who say that our City will never be the same, I say you are right. It will be better.

Now we understand much more clearly why people from all over the globe want to come to New York, and to America. . .why they always have, and why they always will.

It's called freedom, equal protection under law, respect for human life, and the promise of opportunity.

They Were All Heroes

All of the victims of this tragedy were innocent.

All of them were heroes.

The Bible says [John 15:13] "Greater love hath no man than this, that a man lay down his life for his friends." Our brave New York City Firefighters . . . New York City Police Officers . . . Port Authority Police Officers . . . EMS workers . . . health care workers . . . court officers . . . and uniformed service members . . .

They laid down their lives for strangers. They were inspired by their sense of duty and their love for humanity. As they raced into the Twin Towers and the other buildings to save lives, they didn't stop to ask how rich or poor the person was, they didn't stop to ask what religion, what race, what nationality. They just raced in to save their fellow human beings.

They are the best example of love that we have in our society.

The people they were trying to rescue—the people who worked in the World Trade Center and the buildings around it—were each engaged in the quiet heroism of supporting their families, pursuing their dreams and playing their own meaningful part in a diverse, dynamic and free society. They represented more than 60 different nations. They will also occupy a permanent and sacred place in our history and in our hearts.

A Miracle

Even in the midst of the darkest tragedy there are miracles that help our faith to go on. I would like to share one miracle of September 11th with you.

St. Paul's Chapel is one of the oldest and most historic buildings in the City of New York. It was built in 1766, when the surrounding area was still countryside. The Chapel survived our war of independence—including seven years of wartime occupation.

After George Washington was inaugurated the first President of the United States, in New York City on April 30th, 1789, he walked to St. Paul's, and he kneeled down to pray. The pew where he worshipped is still there. Framed on the wall beside it is the oldest known representation of the Great Seal of the United States of America—it's a majestic eagle, holding in one talon an olive branch, proclaiming our abiding desire for peace . . . and in the other, a cluster of arrows, a forewarning of our determination to defend our liberty. On a banner above the Eagle is written *E Pluribus Unum,* "Out of Many, One."

For the past 25 years, the chapel stood directly in the shadow of the World Trade Center Towers. When the Towers fell, more than a dozen modern buildings were destroyed and damaged. Yet somehow, amid all the destruction and devastation, St. Paul's Chapel still stands . . . without so much as a broken window.

It's a small miracle in some ways, but the presence of that chapel standing defiant and serene amid the ruins of war sends an eloquent message about the strength and resilience of the people of New York City, and the people of America.

We unite under the banner of *E Pluribus Unum.* We find strength in our diversity. We're a city where people look different, talk different, think different. But we're a City at one with all of the people at the World Trade Center, and with all of America. We love our diversity, and we love our freedom.

The Arrows and Olive Branch

Like our founding fathers who fought and died for freedom
. . . like our ancestors who fought and died to preserve our
union and to end the sin of slavery . . . like our fathers and
grandfathers who fought and died to liberate the world from
Nazism, and Fascism, and Communism . . . the cluster of arrows to defend our freedom, and the olive branch of peace
have now been handed to us.

We will hold them firmly in our hands, honor their memory, and lift them up toward heaven to light the world.

In the days since this attack, we have met the worst of humanity with the best of humanity.

We pray for our President, George W. Bush . . . and for
our Governor George Pataki . . . who have provided us with
such inspiring leadership during these very, very difficult
times. We pray for all of those whose loved ones are lost or
missing . . . we pray for our children, and we say to them:
"Do not be afraid. It's safe to live your life." Finally, we pray
for America . . . and for all of those who join us in defending freedom, law, and humanity.

We humbly bow our heads and we ask God to bless the
City of New York, and we ask God to bless the United States
of America.

"We Stand by You"

Megan Hallinan

> The effects of the attacks on the World Trade Center were felt
> far beyond New York City. Thousands of men and women
> serving in the U.S. military were overseas at the time of the
> attacks. As they watched the video of the planes crashing into
> the towers and the towers' subsequent collapse, many soldiers
> and sailors were frustrated waiting for their mission. Megan
> Hallinan, an ensign aboard the USS *Winston S Churchill*, sent
> an e-mail to her father in which she tells him about a poignant
> and moving incident that raised the spirits of all those aboard
> her ship.

W ell, we are still out at sea, with little direction as to what
our next priority is. The remainder of our port visits,
which were to be centered around max liberty and goodwill
to the United Kingdom, have all but been cancelled. We have
spent every day since the attacks going back and forth within
imaginary boxes drawn in the ocean, standing high-security
watches, and trying to make the best of our time.

New Friends

It hasn't been that fun I must confess, and to be even more
honest, a lot of people are frustrated at the fact that they either can't be home, or we don't have more direction right
now. We have seen the articles and the photographs, and
they are sickening. Being isolated as we are, I don't think
we appreciate the full scope of what is happening back
home, but we are definitely feeling the effects. About two

hours ago the junior officers were called to the bridge to conduct Ship handling drills. We were about to do a man overboard drill when we got a call from the *Lutjens* (D185), a German warship that was moored ahead of us on the pier in Plymouth, England. While in port, the *Winston S Churchill* and the *Lutjens* got together for a sports day/cookout on our fantail, and we made some pretty good friends. Now at sea they called over on bridge-to-bridge, requesting to pass us close up on our port side, to say goodbye.

We prepared to render them honors on the bridge wing, and the Captain told the crew to come topside to wish them farewell. As they were making their approach, our Conning Officer announced through her binoculars that they were flying an American flag. As they came even closer, we saw that it was flying at half-mast. The bridge wing was crowded with people as the Boatswain's Mate blew two whistles— Attention to Port—the ship came up alongside and we saw that the entire crew of the German ship were manning the rails, in their dress blues. They had made up a sign that was displayed on the side that read "We Stand by You."

Needless to say there was not a dry eye on the bridge as they stayed alongside us for a few minutes and we cut our salutes. It was probably the most powerful thing I have seen in my entire life and more than a few of us fought to retain our composure. It was a beautiful day outside today. We are no longer at liberty to divulge over unsecure e-mail our location, but we could not have asked for a finer day at sea. The German Navy did an incredible thing for this crew, and it has truly been the highest point in the days since the attacks. It's amazing to think that only a half-century ago things were quite different, and to see the unity that is being demonstrated throughout Europe and the world makes us all feel proud to be out here doing our job. After the ship pulled away and we prepared to begin our man overboard drills the Officer of the Deck turned to me and said "I'm staying Navy." I'll write you when I know more about when I'll be home, but for now, this is probably the best news that I could send you. Love you guys.

Renewed Patriotism

Michele Wallace Campanelli

> Immediately after the attacks of September 11, 2001, Americans began to feel a renewed sense of patriotism and pride in their country. Houses and businesses everywhere began flying the American flag; businesses put up signs reading "God Bless America" and "United We Stand." Bumper stickers with similar sayings and magnetic flags soon appeared on cars and trucks. Author Michele Wallace Campanelli writes in the following essay about her search for an American flag.

Flags were flying on every house down my block when I realized that my husband and I, who had recently bought our first home, didn't have a flag of our own. Donating blood and money no longer felt like enough.

A Quest

Immediately, I left on a quest to find an American flag to show my patriotic spirit. After starting up my ancient car, I headed to the local Kmart, Wal-Mart, Home Depot, Lowes, Ace Hardware and even some craft stores. Everywhere I was told the same thing: "We had flags this morning, but we're sold out now. Come back next week, and we'll have more flags."

Next week? Somehow next week didn't seem good enough for this fervent patriot.

I hurried back to my car to proceed to plan B—trying to buy a flag over the Internet. As I drove down the highway, I noticed that nearly every marquee announced, "God Bless

From "The Aftermath," by Michele Wallace Campanelli, in *Chicken Soup for the Soul of America: Stories to Heal the Heart of Our Nation*, edited by Jack Canfield, Mark Victor Hansen, and Matthew E. Adams (Deerfield Beach, FL: Health Communications, Inc., 2002). Copyright © 2002 by Michele Wallace Campanelli. Reprinted with permission.

America" or "United We Stand." Cars passed me with flag stickers on the bumpers or small flags tied to antennas. Some cars even had flags draped over luggage racks. This drive was unlike any other I had ever taken. I had known before that Americans were proud, but seeing so many flags today, displayed in such diverse ways, hit me differently than on any Fourth of July or President's Day. This varied display of the nation's colors spoke of unity, courage, determination.

As I stopped at a red light, I heard a familiar tune drifting from a breakfast shop that had opened its doors to welcome customers. "The Star-Spangled Banner" was blasting from a loud speaker.

". . . O say does that star-spangled banner
Yet wave!
O'er the land of the free
And the home of the brave!"

A chill ran down my spine. Although I had heard the words a thousand times before, this day I truly appreciated how Francis Scott Key must have felt as he wrote them. What a welcome sight is the red, white and blue banner flying high. Even though the light had turned green, the cars around me didn't speed off. The lady in the car next to me wiped her eyes and gave me a nod before proceeding on her way. Today, Americans were different, changed. The horror meant to divide us somehow did not. Instead, we were uniting through this tragedy, proud of our heritage.

Still Searching

When I got home I searched the Internet for Old Glory online. I surfed markets in other countries: China, Europe and Australia. Everywhere I searched notices were posted: "Seamstresses working overtime." "Sorry for the delay." "None currently available." All over the world, the American flag supply seemed to have run out.

Still determined, I called family members and asked if they knew where I could find a flag. All were flying their own or didn't know where new ones could be found. My mission seemed hopeless.

Hours passed.

Suddenly, a knock sounded on my door. My grandfather, Jim Pauline, a man who had served in the United States Army during World War II in the tank division at Normandy under General Patton, held out his hands. In them lay Old Glory.

"Thought you might want this," Grandpa smiled. "Sorry it isn't very big."

This Is War

Many Americans were angered by the attacks of September 11, 2001, and wanted revenge on those responsible. Ann Coulter, a syndicated columnist, wrote a column for the conservative publication National Review Online *in which she expressed sentiments many Americans were feeling at the time. Shortly after her article appeared, she was fired by the magazine.*

The nation has been invaded by a fanatical, murderous cult. And we welcome them. We are so good and so pure we would never engage in discriminatory racial or "religious" profiling.

People who want our country destroyed live here, work for our airlines, and are submitted to the exact same airport shakedown as a lumberman from Idaho. . . .

Airports scrupulously apply the same laughably ineffective airport harassment to Suzy Chapstick as to Muslim hijackers. It is preposterous to assume every passenger is a potential crazed homicidal maniac. We know who the homicidal maniacs are. They are the ones cheering and dancing right now.

We should invade their countries, kill their leaders and convert them to Christianity. We weren't punctilious about locating and punishing only Hitler and his top officers. We carpet-bombed German cities; we killed civilians. That's war. And this is war.

Ann Coulter, "This Is War," *National Review Online,* September 13, 2001, www.nationalreview.com.

I gave him a hug. Even if the flag was just a foot long, I didn't care. The size of the flag couldn't measure the love that I have for my country and for the family and friends who live within its borders.

The Flag's Meaning

I walked out into my yard and among the dozens that flew already, I added my very own treasured banner. It seemed a simple gesture, but the meaning was so profound it brought tears to my eyes. I used to think the flag was the symbol of our country, but I now know that what Congress decided on June 14, 1777, rings as true today as it did 224 years ago:

The stars represent each of the United States.

The blue field behind the stars stands for vigilance, perseverance and justice.

The white stripes reflect purity and innocence.

The red stripes symbolize valor and courage.

The terrorist bombers may have murdered five thousand innocent Americans on September 11, 2001, but they couldn't destroy our American spirit.

Approximately eighty-eight thousand flags were purchased in the days after the terrorist attacks—more than at any other time in history. My quest to find a flag wasn't easy. I wasn't alone in wanting to show pride for this beloved country. And for that, I am eternally grateful.

God bless America!

Neighborly Concern

Elizabeth Grove

Shocked by the attacks on their city, Americans, and New Yorkers in particular, underwent a sudden and dramatic transformation. People became nicer and more polite to each other. They nodded at strangers and became tolerant on motorways infamous for aggravating commutes. Elizabeth Grove, who lives in Brooklyn Heights, a New York City neighborhood, explains what it was like living in New York after September 11 and how total strangers were cheered when they saw their neighbors were safe after the attacks.

For years I've been answering the question "You live *in* New York City? Like, right *in* New York City?" I live in Brooklyn Heights, but this is a distinction meaningful only to those with 100- zip code prefixes, so I would say yes and try to explain. It wasn't what they thought, I would say, it's not a swirling mass of faceless commuters, steel and pollution, lawless thugs, sci-fi androids, wreaking havoc while misplaced demi-Americans like me ran for cover from submachine gun fire, clutching dry cleaning and loaves of bread. It's not what you think, I would say. OK, there were days where it seemed like that. But, I would say, really, it's just like any other small town.

Like Any Other Small Town

It was a partial lie, of course, the unspoken, ". . . with really good restaurants, important museums, significant theater, and the financial pulse of the world . . ." hanging heavy in

Excerpted from "I'm So Glad You're Alive," by Elizabeth Grove, in *Before and After: Stories from New York*, edited by Thomas Beller (New York: Mr. Beller's Neighborhood Books, 2002). Copyright © 2002 by Thomas Beller. Reprinted with permission.

the air. We liked having it both ways: little town and power capital. Let's face it, in most New Yorkers' derisive "Middle America" slurring was included everything besides Los Angeles, San Francisco, the college town where they may have spent four years, and Seattle after Kurt Cobain.

Still, no one lives in a city of eight million. We live in villages, in many cases smaller, more provincial and more proscriptive than the little backwaters we allude to like we know what we're talking about. But in the days since September 11, we've been shell-shocked, knocked down, and made earnest. Sadly, our blood isn't needed right now and it turns out most of us don't have viable disaster skills. Volunteering at Long Island College Hospital that first day, I answered no to three questions—Did I have a car? A medical background? Know CPR?—and was given a sweet smile and a number to call on an hourly basis. Days two and three I wondered why I had never learned to weld.

Clearly, I am not alone. And that left many of us with little to do but bear witness and simply populate the city, our mere presence, our one hundred, one hundred and fifty, two hundred pounds, whatever, anchoring the city in the way the World Trade Center once did. This close to the blast site, with its mountain of rubble burning and, even in total collapse, still higher than the Washington Monument, there is little joy in being alive while it sinks in and sinks in and sinks in and we understand war is coming. But there is the accident and the necessity of being alive and somehow letting everyone know it. And we seem to be doing it by joining the rest of the country, our de facto secessionist tendencies wiped away by grief, our small town sentiments aroused by fear, and our notions of what it means to be a Rockwellian American filtered through the lens of what is still New York City.

Changes

If you somehow impossibly woke up on Day Two or Day Three and didn't know what had happened, you would have wondered where you were living. Strangers nodded as they passed on the street, beat cops stood on every corner and people came up to them to shake their hands or pat them on the backs. No car horns honked. When you went into stores, inquiries were made about your family and friends. Everyone safe? Doors were held. Lampposts were covered in notices about church services, synagogue services, mosque services, ecumenical services.

Downtown there were more signs: The Blood Center Has Reached Capacity. Thank You. Please Try Again Next Week. Flags flew from every stationary and moving object: homes, storefronts, cars, people. At the candlelight vigil on the Promenade on Thursday night there were more flags, prayer, fewer renditions of, say, "My Sweet Lord" than "The Star Spangled Banner."

We fell in love with our mayor.

Had we not had been preoccupied with sorrow, rage, fear, and the sudden unfurling of history, we would've noticed sooner how weird this was. We're walking the streets and lighting candles and talking politics not so altered we don't know how altered we are. But too altered to really understand what it means to be here on September 11, 12, 13, 14, 15, 16 . . .

There is nothing wrong with this. Nothing except it's all so wrong. Not in its essence. We are Americans living in America. Even if our streets, cosmetically speaking, seldom resemble the America we think we know, you know, that America, there's nothing foolish about emulating the aspects that, once scorned, suddenly seem comforting.

But because it's a transformation informed utterly and completely by evil so profound most of us haven't yet even scratched the surface of it, it can't help but bring with it a certain shadow-self sensibility. From this, we've produced not an accurate image, but instead a retina image of a small town we think we can recall or become, that we can see when we close our eyes instead of the vision of two big bullets filled with human shrapnel, instead of the World Trade Center burning hellishly and falling straight down like a KO'd brain-dead boxer.

At our core, we are already a real community, which is what this is all about, and we always have been. At the pettiest level, most of us don't even have enough square feet to make spending a lot of time at home a comfortable option. We're out and about and rubbing elbows and rubbing each other the wrong way, and more often the right way. Confronted with lesser evils, we've come together in the face of them time and time again. There are shopkeepers, people on the subway platform, neighbors we know and who know us. The sane and loving, and there are millions of us, have always found their ways to one another.

Neighborly Concern

In the late sixties there was a children's book, *Maxie,* set in New York City. Maxie was an old woman who felt useless (and if written now, clinically depressed . . .) so she decided not to get out of bed one morning. Before long the entire neighborhood was on her doorstep. One neighbor always woke up from the sound of Maxie's slippers on the floor and had overslept. Another knew to leave for work when Maxie's too tightly sprung window shade shot up. Others set time by Maxie's teakettle, from her bird chirping when she fed him, when she got her newspaper and her bottle of milk, and so on. This being New York, they surrounded her bed—rather menacingly, to my child's mind—with concern and not a little irritation. So Maxie got out of bed.

My friend, Angela, had her concerns about a neighbor in the days following the blast. He'd moved in across the street, and had a bright florescent light, so she was always aware of when he was home and she could see him as he moved around the apartment with his shades up. His lights, she said, hadn't been on since at least Tuesday. Sitting on her stoop, after the candlelight vigil on the Promenade, we watched his dark windows.

Then he came home. A man entered the building and a moment later the lights on the third floor flipped on. We sat there cheering, feeling this small joy over a stranger we didn't know by name or face, by occupation or anything else, but whose absence we had noted. We imagined, only half-jokingly going up to him and saying, we're so glad you're alive. Chances are he wasn't anywhere near the blast. But chances are he would understand.

As I write, there are plenty of lights that are not flipping on, and plenty of people feeling the pain of that, up close, or across streets, across the country and the world, people who are known or not known but who are grieved. If we are transforming ourselves, and clearly we irrevocably and inevitably are, it needn't be in parody, grotesque or otherwise, and it needn't be conjured from sheer shock and reaction. New York is not a small town, not the kind we imagine exists somewhere free from cruelty or isolation but plump with kindness and old-fashioned virtue. The flags will probably fall away or be waved for war instead of the complicated ways they're waving now, car horns will sound again, and we'll witness or perpetuate any number of little or big incivilities. But the sentiment in this new city is not a bad one these days: I'm so glad you're alive.

When you come right down to it, and New York City has, it's the only sentiment that matters. And that's not just about small town America or just about big town America or just about America at all.

Racist Assumptions

Bob Levey

> After the Japanese attacked Pearl Harbor in 1941, the U.S.
> government authorized the roundup and internment of thou-
> sands of Americans of Japanese descent. The Japanese Amer-
> icans were sent to desolate camps in the western United
> States where they remained for the remainder of World
> War II. The detainments were an outright case of racism and
> xenophobia. It was feared that even though they were Ameri-
> can citizens, the Japanese Americans would support Japan—
> either covertly or openly—during the war.
>
> Some Americans felt the same fears about other ethnicities
> when Iranians captured Americans and held them as hostages
> during the late 1970s, and again after the bombing of Okla-
> homa City in 1995 which was initially blamed on Islamic
> extremists. After the attacks of September 11, many Arab
> Americans were afraid they would be blamed by other Ameri-
> cans for the terrorists' actions, and indeed, *Washington Post*
> columnist Bob Levey witnessed a confrontation between an
> Arab American man and a non–Arab American woman
> aboard the city's subway train. As Levey argues, the war on
> terrorism cannot be won if Americans continue to judge oth-
> ers based on their race or ethnicity.

When you've finally turned off the TV because you
can't stand any more, when the front door is locked
and the cat is fed and the night sky is utterly silent, it's just
you and your thoughts.

Late Tuesday night [September 11, 2001] I recalled my

father, about 50 years ago, telling me for the first time about Pearl Harbor.

He described the clenched jaws he saw that afternoon on the streets of New York, the disbelief on every face, the astonishment at how life can deal from the bottom of the deck. And then, after about 24 hours, he saw resolve. Not just to get mad or get even or both. The resolve to go forward by upholding our country's best traditions, our very reasons for existing.

The Confrontation

On the Red Line Wednesday morning, about 24 hours after the horrors of Sept. 11, I saw what I had feared I would see.

A man was sitting near the back door of the fourth car. He was wearing a suit and tie. He was reading *The Washington Post*. He was obviously of Arab extraction.

A woman sat across from him. She was obviously not of Arab extraction.

She stared at the man for about four stops. She was apparently trying to work up the courage to say something to him. Near Cleveland Park [metro stop], she bolted over and said, accusingly, right in his face, "Why?"

The man was startled. He put down his paper and asked the woman to repeat herself.

"Why? Why did you people do this?"

The man's face flashed through fear, anger, caution, confusion. He said, very calmly, in perfect, unaccented English, "Ma'am, I am an American citizen. I am just as upset as you are."

But of course, what he really meant was, "Please don't blame me or harm me just because I am obviously of Arab extraction."

I fear that many more such confrontations are coming.

I can't imagine a repeat of the internment camps of World War II. In an age of Big Media, in an America that's far more diverse than it was 60 years ago, no broad-brush "security step" could last a day, much less get started.

No, I'm far more worried about the small-scale sort of

thing I saw on the subway (and saw aboard a Metrobus in the late 1970s, the day after Iranians kidnapped several dozen employees of the U.S. Embassy).

This isn't the horrid, vicious racism of lynchings and church bombings. But it is just as profound and just as corrosive.

It damns first and asks questions later.

It is dangerously ignorant of our history and our glory.

It is especially galling in a city as varied and as sophisticated as Washington.

Kids and Race

Ask your kids about the reflex I saw in the subway. Ask them whether, when they take the measure of someone, they see skin color first, or a swarthy complexion, or a nose that is or isn't broad.

If they are smart—and kids are always smart—they will tell you that race is another generation's hang-up, that it doesn't take you inside someone's soul. When it comes to race, they'll tell you, they aren't their fathers' Oldsmobiles.

A 15-year-old called me Tuesday afternoon.

He is Iranian American. He said he was scared to death when he first heard the awful news.

He feared retaliation against himself and his family.

However, he began to feel a lot better shortly after he got home from school. One by one, his buddies from West Springfield [Virginia] High School (all of them white) called to dissect the disastrous day with him.

Not one referred to Arabs as a group or tried to lay the events at his or their doorstep. "It made me feel wonderful," the boy said.

But then, the father of one friend jumped on the line and ordered the conversation terminated right away. The father didn't explain, "but I think I know why," this 15-year-old said.

I think I know why, too.

It makes my skin crawl.

This boy was born at Inova Fairfax Hospital. He has spent his entire life in Northern Virginia. He told me he wears

Nike sneakers and a faded University of Virginia sweat shirt, like thousands of other kids.

But now he is being judged by his ethnic origin—before the judge even knows whether Arabs were responsible for the horrors of Tuesday.

You will hear an awful lot over the next weeks about how we Americans must come together.

You will see huge increases in church attendance.

You will read stories about people who donate blood six times.

You will see gas station owners who try to charge $5 a gallon shouted back down to $1.45.

But I hope you'll hear shouts, too, about the fundamental strength of our country: the pot that melts us all.

If we are going to summon the will to beat terrorism, we need to check our underpinning first. It won't be very sturdy if we judge books by their covers.

We're All in This Together

My father made much the same point in that conversation we had 50 years ago.

He told me about an Irish Catholic fellow who clapped him on the back as they stood on a midtown Manhattan street corner on Dec. 7, 1941.

This man never asked my father if he was Irish, Catholic or Martian. He just said they were all in this together, and they'd all have to stand or fall as one.

True then. True now.

Chapter 4

The Arab World's

Response

Chapter Preface

W hen the Jewish State of Israel was formed in 1948, it was carved out of a historic region in the Middle East known as Palestine. Arabs and Jews had been fighting over territory in the Middle East for decades before the establishment of Israel. After World War II, the United Nations proposed a plan to partition Palestine into Arab and Jewish states. Even though the Palestinians rejected the partition, the United Nations created a Jewish homeland known as the State of Israel. Soon after, thousands of Arab Palestinians fled to neighboring Islamic countries rather than live in a Jewish state. Israel was immediately attacked by its Islamic neighbors (Egypt, Syria, Lebanon, Jordan, and Iraq), but was able to repel the invaders. The clashes between Israelis and Palestinians continued into the twenty-first century in a never-ending spiral of violence and retaliation. During Israel's first and subsequent wars with its surrounding Islamic neighbors, the United States always supported Israel and its right to exist. Thus, it is no surprise that Palestinians and Arabs resent the United States and its power.

While the Western world was almost universally shocked and angered by the attacks on the United States on September 11, 2001, much of the Arab world held divergent views. Many Arab newspapers published articles in which they alleged that the Jews, Zionists, Israelis, and even the Americans themselves were responsible for the attacks of September 11. According to their circuitous reasoning, the attacks on the United States were an attempt to make the world hate Arabs.

Other Arabs blamed American foreign policy in the Middle East for the attacks. They asserted that the United States deserved to be attacked because of its unconditional support of Israel. The Palestinians claim that they themselves are the victims of terrorist attacks by the Israelis, and they gloried in the fact that now the United States understands what it is like to be a victim of terror. A few Islamic leaders, known as mullahs, even spoke out in approval of the attacks. They, like Osama bin Laden, reasoned that Islam permits, even encourages, a Muslim who is under attack by an enemy to strike back. Many Muslims in the Middle East contend that the United States, through its allies, foreign policy decisions, and its support of Israel, is killing Muslims in Palestine, Kashmir, Chechnya, and Iraq, so it is right and just that Muslims strike back.

Other Islamic scholars argue that Islam does not endorse or condone the killing of innocent people and that the Koran, the Islamic bible, specifically forbids terrorism and murder. Many mullahs contend that bin Laden's calls for a jihad (holy war) against the United States are invalid and that Muslims should ignore them. Furthermore, they argue that the terrorists do not represent Islam and bin Laden should not be allowed to start a war between Islam and the West.

With such conflicting views about Islam and what it allows and encourages, it is no wonder that Westerners are confused about the Arab response to the attacks.

"Hypocrisy Rears Its Ugly Head"

Osama bin Laden

> Osama bin Laden, a Saudi Arabian exile living in
> Afghanistan, is reputed to be the leader of a terrorist organi-
> zation known as al-Qaeda. Evidence points to bin Laden and
> al-Qaeda as responsible for planning and carrying out the
> attacks on the World Trade Center in 1993, the bombings of
> the U.S. embassies in Kenya and Tanzania in 1998, and the
> bombing of the USS *Cole* in 2000. Bin Laden is also believed
> to have organized the terrorist attacks of September 11, 2001.
> Bin Laden feels that the presence of U.S. troops on Arabian
> soil and American support for Israel are affronts to Islam and
> he has made it his mission to force the withdrawal of the
> American presence from the Middle East.
>
> On October 7, 2001, the United States and its allies began
> bombing Afghanistan in retaliation for harboring bin Laden
> and al-Qaeda. That night a videotape of bin Laden denounc-
> ing the United States was shown on al-Jazeera, a television
> station based in Qatar. It is believed that bin Laden made the
> videotape before the bombing began and had it delivered to
> the television station with instructions to show it once the
> expected U.S.-led retaliation started. In this selection, taken
> from a transcript of the videotape, bin Laden does not admit
> to planning the attacks, but tells his audience the United
> States deserved the attacks because of its hypocrisy. Innocent
> Muslim children are killed every day due to U.S. policies and
> no one protests their deaths. He concludes by telling Ameri-
> cans they will not be able to live in peace and security until
> Arabs reclaim their own lands.

From "Hypocrisy Rears Its Ugly Head," by Osama bin Laden, *Washington Post*, October 8, 2001.

149

I bear witness that there is no God but Allah and that Muhammad is his messenger.

There is America, hit by God in one of its softest spots. Its greatest buildings were destroyed, thank God for that. There is America, full of fear from its north to its south, from its west to its east. Thank God for that.

What America Deserves

What America is tasting now is something insignificant compared to what we have tasted for scores of years. Our nation [the Islamic world] has been tasting this humiliation and this degradation for more than 80 years. Its sons are killed, its blood is shed, its sanctuaries are attacked, and no one hears and no one heeds.

When God blessed one of the groups of Islam, vanguards of Islam, they destroyed America. I pray to God to elevate their status and bless them.

Millions of innocent children are being killed as I speak. They are being killed in Iraq without committing any sins, and we don't hear condemnation or a *fatwa* [religious decree] from the rulers. In these days, Israeli tanks infest Palestine—in Jenin, Ramallah, Rafah, Beit Jala and other places in the land of Islam—and we don't hear anyone raising his voice or moving a limb.

When the sword comes down [on America], after 80 years, hypocrisy rears its ugly head. They deplore and they lament for those killers, who have abused the blood, honor and sanctuaries of Muslims. The least that can be said about those people is that they are debauched. They have followed injustice. They supported the butcher over the victim, the oppressor over the innocent child. May God show them his wrath and give them what they deserve.

A Clear Situation

I say that the situation is clear and obvious. After this event, after the senior officials have spoken in America, starting with the head of infidels worldwide, President George W. Bush, and those with him. They have come out in force with their men and have turned even the countries that belong to Islam to this treachery, and they want to wag their tail at God, to fight Islam, to suppress people in the name of terrorism. When people at the ends of the earth, Japan, were killed by their hundreds of thousands, young and old, it was not considered a war crime, it is something that has justification. Millions of children in Iraq is something that has justification. But when they lose dozens of people in Nairobi and Dar es Salaam [capitals of Kenya and Tanzania, where U.S. embassies were bombed in 1998], Iraq was struck and Afghanistan was struck. Hypocrisy stood in force behind the head of infidels worldwide, behind the cowards of this age, America and those who are with it.

These events have divided the whole world into two sides—the side of believers and the side of infidels. May God keep you away from them. Every Muslim has to rush to make his religion victorious. The winds of faith have come. The winds of change have come to eradicate oppression from the island of Muhammad, peace be upon him.

To America, I say only a few words to it and its people. I swear by God, who has elevated the skies without pillars, neither America nor the people who live in it will dream of security before we live it in Palestine, and not before all the infidel armies leave the land of Muhammad, peace be upon him.

God is great, may pride be with Islam. May peace and God's mercy be upon you.

No Tears for America

Muhammad Abbas

In 2000, Muhammad Abbas wrote an article for the Egyptian
newspaper *Al-Sha'ab* in which he attacked the Ministry of
Culture for publishing a book, *Feast of Seaweed*, that Islam
considered heretical. His article prompted students to riot and
the newspaper was shut down by the government for a few
months.

After the September 11 attacks, Abbas wrote another column for *Al-Sha'ab*. In this article, excerpted below, Abbas
says he cannot cry over the American loss of life because his
tears have run dry crying for Palestinian martyrs and those
who have died at the hands of Americans. He is glad that
Americans have finally learned that they, too, are vulnerable
to pain, fear, and death. He notes that it is impossible for
Americans to protect themselves against martyrs who are
willing to die and warns that chemical, biological, and even
nuclear bombs are potential weapons in this holy war.

I would have liked . . . to add to the flood of crocodile tears
flowing from the four corners of the earth, as an expression of sorrow for America's victims . . . but I have found
that my reservoir of tears ran dry a hundred years ago. . . .
Perhaps in [yet] another hundred years the time will come
for me to cry over five thousand or even fifty thousand slain
Americans.

Did I say five thousand? Did I say fifty thousand? By Allah, this number is miniscule. . . .

The tyrants of the world and of history (i.e. the Ameri-

Excerpted from "Special Dispatch No. 280: Terror in America (11): Egyptian Islamists:
The U.S. Will Be Targeted with Nonconventional Weapons; Americans Working in the
Middle East Will Be Attacked," by Muhammad Abbas, *Al-Sha'ab*, October 3, 2001. Copy-
right © 2001 by The Middle East Media Research Institute. Reprinted with permission.

cans) suddenly discovered that their leader too could be attacked, and that the white Christian man can scream, suffer pain, bleed, and die. . . .

Do you want me to cry, right this minute, over two or three buildings? By Allah, that's ridiculous. How can someone who knows how you destroyed countries and obliterated cities from the face of the earth be sorry about two buildings. . . .

The Power of Allah

Despite all this, I did not exult. Death has glory and majesty, even when it is a dog that dies, let alone five thousand souls. I sat in front of the television and tears filled my eyes. I admit, I did not cry out of sympathy [for the victims]; [I cried] out of fear of Allah the powerful, the precious, the victor, the avenger, the just; how he takes the tyrants just when they think they rule the Earth and are capable of confronting Him. . . .

Islam is alive and well. The hero martyrs in Palestine are the ones who showed the world the incredible potential of the martyr's body. Whoever the perpetrators of the act [in the U.S.] may be, Islam is their teacher and their professor. . . .

The genius of what happened is in its successful transformation from theory to practice. If people are willing to sacrifice their lives, how can America defend itself from these ambulatory human bombs who at any given moment, anywhere, can . . . cause a truck and a train to collide, set a gas station alight, and set off chemical, biological, and even atomic bombs?

When writing this article, I was surprised to discover an article I wrote years ago, in which I warned America that going too far with its oppression would lead to its destruction, and that within a few short years it would be taken by surprise by atom bombs exploding in New York, Chicago, and California. . . . That is what I said [then], and behold, it has come to pass. . . . Additional operations are a certainty, and [they are] an inevitable response to American repression and tyranny. . . . The U.S. will collapse from within, as did the U.S.S.R.

Americans Are Terrorists

Sulaiman Abu Ghaith

Sulaiman Abu Ghaith is a spokesman for al-Qaeda, the terrorist organization run by Osama bin Laden. In a videotape broadcast October 10, 2001, on al-Jazeera, a television station based in Qatar, Abu Ghaith declares that the United States has declared war on Islam and all Muslims have been suffering as a result. The United States has been engaging in its own form of terrorism against Islam; therefore, the attacks against America were simply Islam taking its revenge. He asserts that the battle against the United States will not end until American influence is eradicated from the Middle East. The war between Islam and America is a battle between infidels and true believers and it is up to Muslims to defend their faith against the Americans.

Peace be upon Muhammad our prophet and those who follow him. I direct this message to the entire Islamic nation, and I say to them that all sides today have come together against the nation of Islam and the Muslims.

Islam Has Been Suffering

This is the crusade that [President George W.] Bush has promised us, coming toward Afghanistan against the Islamic nation and the Afghan people. We are living under this bombardment from the crusade, which is also targeting the whole Islamic community.

Excerpted from Sulaiman Abu Ghaith's statement as a spokesman for the al-Qaeda network, October 10, 2001.

We have a fair and just case. The Islamic nation, for more than 80 years, has been suffering. The Palestinian people have been living under the Jewish and Zionist occupation; nobody moves to help them. Here we are, this is an Arab land, this is a land that is being desecrated, people have come to take its wealth.

The nation must know that terror, and the terror of the United States, is only a ploy. Is it possible that America and its allies would kill and that would not be called terrorism? And when the victim comes out to take revenge, it is called terrorism. This must not be acceptable.

America must know that the nation will not keep quiet any more and will not allow what happens against it. Jihad [holy war] today is a religious duty of every Muslim, if they haven't got an excuse. God says fight, for the sake of God and to uphold the name of God.

The American interests are everywhere all over the world. Every Muslim has to play his real and true role to uphold his religion and his nation in fighting, and jihad is a duty. . . .

A Good Deed

I want to talk on another point: that those youths who did what they did and destroyed America with their airplanes did a good deed. They have moved the battle into the heart of America. America must know that the battle will not leave its land, God willing, until America leaves our land, until it stops supporting Israel, until it stops the blockade against Iraq.

The Americans must know that the storm of airplanes will not stop, God willing, and there are thousands of young people who are as keen about death as Americans are about life.

The Americans must know that by invading the land of Afghanistan they have opened a new page of enmity and struggle between us and the forces of the unbelievers. We will fight them with the material and the spiritual strength that we have, and our faith in God. We shall be victorious.

The Americans have opened a door that will never be

closed. At the end, I address the sons and the young Muslims, the men and women, for them to take their responsibility. The land of Afghanistan and the holy warriors are being subjected to a full crusade with the objective of getting rid of the Islamic nation.

The nation must take up its response and in the end I thank God for allowing us to start this jihad. This battle is a decisive battle between faithlessness and faith. And I ask God to give us victory in the face of our enemy and return them defeated.

A Vision of Plane Crashes

Osama bin Laden

The following selection is a transcription of a videotape of Osama bin Laden talking about the attacks on the World Trade Center and the Pentagon with several of his supporters, including an unidentified Saudi Arabian sheik (Shaykh), during an informal dinner in Kandahar, Afghanistan, in mid-November 2001. All members of the dinner party were aware that their comments were being taped. The videotape begins with the second half of bin Laden's dinner meeting with the sheik, followed by an earlier visit by Taliban (the religious government of Afghanistan) forces to a downed U.S. helicopter in the Ghazni province of Afghanistan, and ends with the beginning of bin Laden's meal with the sheik. U.S. government officials theorize that the original recording on the tape was the visit to the helicopter and that the camera operator began taping the sheik's meeting with bin Laden halfway through the tape. When the tape ran out, the operator rewound the tape to the beginning and recorded the last half of the dinner over the helicopter scenes.

In this selection, the sheik praises bin Laden for the success of the attacks and tells him that Islam has many new converts due to the attacks. In previous statements, bin Laden has denied personal responsibility for the September 11, 2001, attacks against the United States, but in this videotape, he claims to have known about the attacks days before they occurred.

The tape was found by Afghan Northern Alliance forces in

Excerpted from a transcript of videotape of Osama bin Laden meeting with his followers. Released by the U.S. Department of Defense, December 13, 2001.

a home in Jalabad, Afghanistan, after Taliban and al-Qaeda leaders were forced to flee the city. The tape was transcribed by two independent Arabic specialists and the results were compared and confirmed by government translators. There were no inconsistencies in the translation.

Shaykh: (. . . *inaudible* . . .) You have given us weapons, you have given us hope and we thank Allah for you. We don't want to take much of your time, but this is the arrangement of the brothers. People now are supporting us more, even those ones who did not support us in the past, support us more now. I did not want to take that much of your time. We praise Allah, we praise Allah. We came from Kabul. We were very pleased to visit. May Allah bless you both at home and the camp. We asked the driver to take us, it was a night with a full moon, thanks be to Allah. Believe me it is not in the countryside. The elderly . . . everybody praises what you did, the great action you did, which was first and foremost by the grace of Allah. This is the guidance of Allah and the blessed fruit of jihad.

The Situation in Saudi Arabia

Osama bin Laden: Thanks to Allah. What is the stand of the Mosques there (*in Saudi Arabia*)?

Shaykh: Honestly, they are very positive. Shaykh Al-Bahrani (*phonetic*) gave a good sermon in his class after the sunset prayers. It was videotaped and I was supposed to carry it with me, but unfortunately, I had to leave immediately.

OBL: The day of the events?

Shaykh: At the exact time of the attack on America, precisely at the time. He (*Bahrani*) gave a very impressive sermon. Thanks be to Allah for his blessings. He (*Bahrani*) was the first one to write at war time. I visited him twice in Al-Qasim.

OBL: Thanks be to Allah.

Shaykh: This is what I asked from Allah. He (*Bahrani*) told the youth: "You are asking for martyrdom and wonder where you should go (*for martyrdom*)?" Allah was inciting them to go. I asked Allah to grant me to witness the truth in front of the unjust ruler. We ask Allah to protect him and give him the martyrdom, after he issued the first fatwa. He was detained for interrogation, as you know. When he was called in and asked to sign, he told them, "don't waste my time, I have another fatwa. If you want me, I can sign both at the same time."

OBL: Thanks be to Allah.

Shaykh: His position is really very encouraging. When I paid him the first visit about a year and half ago, he asked me, "How is Shaykh Bin-Ladin?" He sends you his special regards. As far as Shaykh Sulayman 'Ulwan is concerned, he gave a beautiful fatwa, may Allah bless him. Miraculously, I heard it on the Quran radio station. It was strange because he (*'Ulwan*) sacrificed his position, which is equivalent to a director. It was transcribed word-by-word. The brothers listened to it in detail. I briefly heard it before the noon prayers. He (*'Ulwan*) said this was jihad and those people were not innocent people (*World Trade Center and Pentagon victims*). He swore to Allah. This was transmitted to Shaykh Sulayman Al (('Umar)) Allah bless him.

OBL: What about Shaykh Al-((Rayan))?

Shaykh: Honestly, I did not meet with him. My movements were truly limited.

OBL: Allah bless you. You are welcome.

Shaykh: (*Describing the trip to the meeting*) They smuggled us and then I thought that we would be in different caves inside the mountains so I was surprised at the guest house and that it is very clean and comfortable. Thanks be to Allah, we also learned that this location is safe, by Allah's blessings. The place is clean and we are very comfortable.

OBL: (. . . *Inaudible* . . .) when people see a strong horse and a weak horse, by nature, they will like the strong horse. This is only one goal; those who want people to worship the lord of the people, without following that doctrine, will be following the doctrine of Muhammad, peace be upon him.

True Islam

(OBL quotes several short and incomplete Hadith verses, as follows):

"I was ordered to fight the people until they say there is no god but Allah, and his prophet Muhammad."

"Some people may ask: why do you want to fight us?"

"There is an association between those who say: I believe in one god and Muhammad is his prophet, and those who don't (. . . *inaudible* . . .)

"Those who do not follow the true fiqh.[1] The fiqh of Muhammad, the real fiqh. They are just accepting what is being said at face value."

OBL: Those youth who conducted the operations did not accept any fiqh in the popular terms, but they accepted the fiqh that the prophet Muhammad brought. Those young men (. . . *inaudible* . . .) said in deeds, in New York and Washington, speeches that overshadowed all other speeches made everywhere else in the world. The speeches are understood by both Arabs and non-Arabs—even by Chinese. It is above all the media said. Some of them said that in Holland, at one of the centers, the number of people who accepted Islam during the days that followed the operations were more than the people who accepted Islam in the last eleven years. I heard someone on Islamic radio who owns a school in America say: "We don't have time to keep up with the demands of those who are asking about Islamic books to learn about Islam." This event made people think (*about true Islam*) which benefited Islam greatly.

Shaykh: Hundreds of people used to doubt you and few only would follow you until this huge event happened. Now hundreds of people are coming out to join you. I remember a vision by Shaykh Salih Al-((Shuaybi)). He said: "There will be a great hit and people will go out by hundreds to Afghanistan." I asked him (*Salih*): "To Afghanistan?" He replied, "Yes." According to him, the only ones who stay behind will be the mentally impotent and the liars (*hypocrites*).

---

1. Fiqh means knowledge in Arabic, but it refers to legal rulings of Muslim scholars on Islamic law.

I remembered his saying that hundreds of people will go out to Afghanistan. He had this vision a year ago. This event discriminated between the different types of followers.

More than We Had Hoped

OBL: (. . . *Inaudible* . . .) we calculated in advance the number of casualties from the enemy, who would be killed based on the position of the tower. We calculated that the floors that would be hit would be three or four floors. I was the most optimistic of them all. (. . . *Inaudible* . . .) due to my experience in this field, I was thinking that the fire from the gas in the plane would melt the iron structure of the building and collapse the area where the plane hit and all the floors above it only. This is all that we had hoped for.

Shaykh: Allah be praised.

OBL: We were at (. . . *inaudible* . . .) when the event took place. We had notification since the previous Thursday that the event would take place that day. We had finished our work that day and had the radio on. It was 5:30 P.M. our time. I was sitting with Dr. Ahmad Abu-al-((Khair)). Immediately, we heard the news that a plane had hit the World Trade Center. We turned the radio station to the news from Washington. The news continued and no mention of the attack until the end. At the end of the newscast, they reported that a plane just hit the World Trade Center.

Shaykh: Allah be praised.

OBL: After a little while, they announced that another plane had hit the World Trade Center. The brothers who heard the news were overjoyed by it.

Shaykh: I listened to the news and I was sitting. We didn't . . . we were not thinking about anything, and all of a sudden, Allah willing, we were talking about how come we didn't have anything, and all of a sudden the news came and everyone was overjoyed and everyone until the next day, in the morning, was talking about what was happening and we stayed until four o'clock, listening to the news every time a little bit different, everyone was very joyous and saying "Allah is great," "Allah is great," "We are thankful to Allah,"

"Praise Allah." And I was happy for the happiness of my brothers. That day the congratulations were coming on the phone non-stop. The mother was receiving phone calls continuously. Thank Allah. Allah is great, praise be to Allah.

A Clear Victory

(Quoting the verse from the Quran)

Shaykh: "Fight them, Allah will torture them, with your hands, he will torture them. He will deceive them and he will give you victory. Allah will forgive the believers, he is knowledgeable about everything."

Shaykh: No doubt it is a clear victory. Allah has bestowed on us . . . honor on us . . . and he will give us blessing and more victory during this holy month of Ramadan. And this is what everyone is hoping for. Thank Allah America came out of its caves. We hit her the first hit and the next one will hit her with the hands of the believers, the good believers, the strong believers. By Allah it is a great work. Allah prepares for you a great reward for this work. I'm sorry to speak in your presence, but it is just thoughts, just thoughts. By Allah, who there is no god but him. I live in happiness, happiness . . . I have not experienced, or felt, in a long time. I remember, the words of Al-Rabbani, he said they made a coalition against us in the winter with the infidels like the Turks, and others, and some other Arabs. And they surrounded us like the days . . . in the days of the prophet Muhammad. Exactly like what's happening right now. But he comforted his followers and said, "This is going to turn and hit them back." And it is a mercy for us. And a blessing to us. And it will bring people back. Look how wise he was. And Allah will give him blessing. And the day will come when the symbols of Islam will rise up and it will be similar to the early days of Al-Mujahedeen and Al-Ansar (*similar to the early years of Islam*). And victory to those who follow Allah. Finally said, if it is the same, like the old days, such as Abu Bakr and Othman and Ali and others. In these days, in our times, that it will be the greatest jihad in the history of Islam and the resistance of the wicked people.

Shaykh: By Allah my Shaykh. We congratulate you for the great work. Thank Allah.

(Tape ends here)

Dreams and Visions

Second segment of Bin Laden's visit, shows up at the front of the tape

OBL: Abdallah Azzam, Allah bless his soul, told me not to record anything (. . . *inaudible* . . .) so I thought that was a good omen, and Allah will bless us (. . . *inaudible* . . .). Abu-Al-Hasan Al-((Masri)), who appeared on Al-Jazeera TV a couple of days ago and addressed the Americans saying: "If you are true men, come down here and face us." (. . . *inaudible* . . .) He told me a year ago: "I saw in a dream, we were playing a soccer game against the Americans. When our team showed up in the field, they were all pilots!" He said: "So I wondered if that was a soccer game or a pilot game? Our players were pilots." He *(Abu-Al-Hasan)* didn't know anything about the operation until he heard it on the radio. He said the game went on and we defeated them. That was a good omen for us.

Shaykh: May Allah be blessed.

Unidentified Man Off Camera: Abd Al Rohman Al-(Ghamri) said he saw a vision, before the operation, a plane crashed into a tall building. He knew nothing about it.

Shaykh: May Allah be blessed!

Sulaiman ((Abu Guaith)): I was sitting with the Shaykh in a room, then I left to go to another room where there was a TV set. The TV broadcasted the big event. The scene was showing an Egyptian family sitting in their living room, they exploded with joy. Do you know when there is a soccer game and your team wins, it was the same expression of joy. There was a subtitle that read: "In revenge for the children of Al Aqsa', Usama Bin Ladin executes an operation against America." So I went back to the Shaykh *(meaning OBL)* who was sitting in a room with 50 to 60 people. I tried to tell him about what I saw, but he made gesture with his hands, meaning: "I know, I know . . ."

Martyrs

OBL: He did not know about the operation. Not everybody knew (. . . *inaudible* . . .). Muhammad ((Atta)) from the Egyptian family *(meaning the Al Qaeda Egyptian group)*, was in charge of the group.

Shaykh: A plane crashing into a tall building was out of anyone's imagination. This was a great job. He was one of the pious men in the organization. He became a martyr. Allah bless his soul.

Shaykh *(Referring to dreams and visions)*: The plane that he saw crashing into the building was seen before by more than one person. One of the good religious people has left everything and come here. He told me, "I saw a vision, I was in a huge plane, long and wide. I was carrying it on my shoulders and I walked from the road to the desert for half a kilometer. I was dragging the plane." I listened to him and I prayed to Allah to help him. Another person told me that last year he saw, but I didn't understand and I told him I don't understand. He said, "I saw people who left for jihad . . . and they found themselves in New York . . . in Washington and New York." I said, "What is this?" He told me the plane hit the building. That was last year. We haven't thought much about it. But, when the incidents happened he came to me and said, "Did you see . . . this is strange." I have another man . . . my god . . . he said and swore by Allah that his wife had seen the incident a week earlier. She saw the plane crashing into a building . . . that was unbelievable, my god.

OBL: The brothers, who conducted the operation, all they knew was that they have a martyrdom operation and we asked each of them to go to America but they didn't know anything about the operation, not even one letter. But they were trained and we did not reveal the operation to them until they are there and just before they boarded the planes.

OBL: (. . . *inaudible* . . .) then he said: Those who were trained to fly didn't know the others. One group of people did not know the other group. (. . . *inaudible* . . .)

(*Someone in the crowd asks OBL to tell the Shaykh about the dream of ((Abu-Da'ud)).*

OBL: We were at a camp of one of the brother's guards in Qandahar. This brother belonged to the majority of the group. He came close and told me that he saw, in a dream, a tall building in America, and in the same dream he saw Mukhtar teaching them how to play karate. At that point, I was worried that maybe the secret would be revealed if everyone starts seeing it in their dream. So I closed the subject. I told him if he sees another dream, not to tell anybody, because people will be upset with him.

"Be Patient"

(*Another person's voice can be heard recounting his dream about two planes hitting a big building*).

OBL: They were overjoyed when the first plane hit the building, so I said to them: be patient.

OBL: The difference between the first and the second plane hitting the towers was twenty minutes. And the difference between the first plane and the plane that hit the Pentagon was one hour.

Shaykh: They (*the Americans*) were terrified thinking there was a coup.

Islamic Law Prohibits Harming the Innocent

Salih bin Muhammad Al-Luheidan

> Osama bin Laden and his supporters claim that their attacks against the United States were justified under Islamic law. Salih bin Muhammad Al-Luheidan, chairman of the Supreme Judicial Council of the Kingdom of Saudi Arabia, disagrees, however. Terrorism and the killing of innocent civilians are prohibited even during times of war; those who perpetrate such acts are guilty of serious crimes under Islamic law, he argues. Under no circumstances can the harming or killing of innocent civilians be condoned by Islamic law or Muslims.

P raise be to God Almighty:
    In the midst of the catastrophic events that have hit America, questions and queries have been raised as to how such acts are judged and interpreted by Islamic Shariah [Law], which encompasses all things and gives clear rulings on every calamity: any calamity that affects humans has its ruling in Islamic Shariah.

Many questions have been raised by officials and by the public as to the ruling of Islamic Shariah on such acts, and whether it is considered acceptable or permissible by Islamic scholars, who shoulder the responsibility of clarifying rulings and Islam's point of view with respect to disasters.

Excerpted from Salih bin Muhammad Al-Luheidan's statement as Saudi Arabian Supreme Judicial Council chairman condemning terrorists acts, September 14, 2001.

Injustice Is Prohibited

God Almighty, the Master of all Rulers, has prohibited injustice among humans. Aggression against those who have committed no crime, and the killing of innocent people, are matters that Islamic Shariah has dealt with: these are not permissible even during wars and invasions. Killing the weak, infants, women, and the elderly, and destroying property, are considered serious crimes in Islam. Acts of corruption and even laying waste to the land, are forbidden by God and by His Prophet. Viewing on the TV networks what happened to the twin towers [of the World Trade Center] was like watching Doomsday.

Those who commit such crimes are the worst of people. Anyone who thinks that any Islamic scholar will condone such acts is totally wrong.

Aggression, injustice and gloating over the kind of crime that we have seen, are totally unacceptable, and forbidden in Islam.

God Almighty says: "And let not the enmity and hatred of others make you avoid justice. Be just, that is nearer to piety." Inflicting a collective punishment is considered by Islam as despicable aggression and perversion. Killing innocent people is by itself a grave crime, quite apart from terrorizing and committing crimes against infants and women. Such acts do no honor to he who commits them, even if he claims to be a Muslim. These sorts of crime are pernicious: in fact, the Kingdom's Islamic scholars, at the time when Saudi Arabia was looking into the phenomenon of hijacking planes, resolved to forbid such acts regardless of the religious belief of the passengers, whether Muslims or non-Muslims, since terrorizing any person is forbidden in Islam.

Despicable Acts

Accordingly it is incumbent upon the Kingdom of Saudi Arabia, as a state governed by the spirit and rulings of Islam, to deplore any criminal and corrupt act, irrespective of whether the perpetrators are Muslims or non-Muslims.

Those who are truly versed in the fundamentals and reality of Islam know that such acts are crimes of endless harm. Considering the numerous questions and queries that arise regarding such acts and our position as a judicial

---

Holy War Against the Americans

Osama bin Laden is the founder and leader of the al-Qaeda organization, a loosely knit network of Islamic extremists and various terrorist organizations that was formed about 1989. Al-Qaeda opposes the continued presence of American military forces in the Middle East following the 1992 Gulf War, U.S. support for Israel, and all governments and institutions that do not follow its interpretation of Islam.

Al-Qaeda is responsible for or has been linked to the 1993 bombing of the World Trade Center, the bombing of U.S. military barracks in Khobar, Saudi Arabia in 1996, the 1998 bombings of the U.S. embassies in Kenya and Tanzania, and the bombing of the USS Cole *in Yemen in 2000.*

Even though bin Laden is not a Muslim scholar (ulema), *he issued a* fatwa *(religious ruling) in 1998 calling for all Muslims to kill Americans—military or civilian—wherever they can be found. Below is an excerpt from the* fatwa.

For over seven years the United States has been occupying the lands of Islam in the holiest of places, the Arabian Peninsula, plundering its riches, dictating to its rulers, humiliating its people, terrorizing its neighbors, and turning its bases in the Peninsula into a spearhead through which to fight the neighboring Muslim peoples.

If some people have in the past argued about the fact of the occupation, all the people of the Peninsula have now acknowledged it. The best proof of this is the Americans' continuing aggression against the Iraqi people using the Peninsula as a staging post, even though all its rulers are against their territories being used to that end, but they are helpless. . . .

If the Americans' aims behind these wars are religious and economic, the aim is also to serve the Jews' petty state and divert attention from its occupation of Jerusalem and murder of Muslims there. The best proof of this is their ea-

board, from an Islamic perspective, we view them as despicable. It has been narrated that the perpetrator alone shall carry the burden of his crimes. I have been telling the press that Muslims do not condone such brutal acts nor should

---

gerness to destroy Iraq, the strongest neighboring Arab state, and their endeavor to fragment all the states of the region such as Iraq, Saudi Arabia, Egypt, and Sudan into paper statelets and through their disunion and weakness to guarantee Israel's survival and the continuation of the brutal crusade occupation of the Peninsula.

All these crimes and sins committed by the Americans are a clear declaration of war on Allah, his messenger, and Muslims. And *ulema* [Muslim Scholars] have throughout Islamic history unanimously agreed that the *jihad* [holy war] is an individual duty if the enemy destroys the Muslim countries. . . .

On that basis, and in compliance with Allah's order, we issue the following *fatwa* [religious ruling] to all Muslims:

The ruling to kill the Americans and their allies—civilians and military—is an individual duty for every Muslim who can do it in any country in which it is possible to do it, in order to liberate the al-Aqsa Mosque and the holy mosque [Mecca] from their grip, and in order for their armies to move out of all the lands of Islam, defeated and unable to threaten any Muslim. This is in accordance with the words of Almighty Allah, "and fight the pagans all together as they fight you all together," and "fight them until there is no more tumult or oppression, and there prevail justice and faith in Allah.". . .

We—with Allah's help—call on every Muslim who believes in Allah and wishes to be rewarded to comply with Allah's order to kill the Americans and plunder their money wherever and whenever they find it. We also call on Muslim ulema, leaders, youths, and soldiers to launch the raid on Satan's U.S. troops and the devil's supporters allying with them, and to displace those who are behind them so that they may learn a lesson.

Osama bin Laden, "Jihad Against Jews and Crusaders," World Islamic Front Statement, February 23, 1998, www.fas.org.

they be held responsible for them, since the creed of Islam urges that no person be responsible for a crime committed by others. This is a prerequisite for justice: "No bearer of burden shall bear the burden of another."

With respect to what has been reported in the media about reactions and how Americans view Arabs and Muslims residing in the United States, I have in the past said that Americans as guardians of democracy cannot deal with Muslims on the basis of crimes committed by a few. Criminals and aggressors cannot be equated with the innocent and the peaceful.

These Acts Cannot Be Condoned

I would like to reiterate that Islam rejects such acts, since it forbids killing of civilians even during times of war, especially if they are not part of the fighting. A religion that views people of the world in such a way cannot in any sense condone such criminal acts, which require that their perpetrators and those who support them are held accountable. As a human community we have to be vigilant and careful to preempt these evils.

Islamic Shariah is based on the principle that prevention is better than treatment; one of its goals is looking into causes.

I would like to confirm that the Islamic World and its religious and political leadership cannot condone such acts; and I am convinced that western and American society cannot deal with Islamic nations and peoples from the basis of the crime committed.

Muslims have to deal in good faith with those who live beside them in all societies, since Islam does not discriminate between humans: for they are all brothers.

This barbaric act is not justified by any sane mindset, or any logic; nor by the religion of Islam. This act is pernicious and shameless and evil in the extreme.

I pray to God to guide the devious to the path of righteousness, and to protect us from all evils and from our own bad deeds, and to be gracious to us.

Appendix: The Evidence Against Osama bin Laden and al-Qaeda

Many Arabs did not believe that Osama bin Laden was responsible for the attacks against the United States on September 11, 2001. In part to convince them of bin Laden's responsibility, the British government released a document in October 2001—and updated it a month later—that summarized the evidence against bin Laden and his al-Qaeda network. Prime Minister Tony Blair told members of Parliament that the evidence was overwhelming and there was no doubt that bin Laden and al-Qaeda were responsible for the attacks.

The following document is a compendium of facts about bin Laden, his al-Qaeda network, their previous attacks against the United States, and their attacks on September 11, 2001.

This document does not purport to provide a prosecutable case against Usama Bin Laden in a court of law. Intelligence often cannot be used evidentially, due both to the strict rules of admissibility and to the need to protect the safety of sources. But on the basis of all the information available Her Majesty's Government (HMG) is confident of its conclusions as expressed in this document.

1. The clear conclusions reached by the government are:

• Usama Bin Laden and Al Qaida, the terrorist network which he heads, planned and carried out the atrocities on 11 September 2001;

• Usama Bin Laden and Al Qaida retain the will and resources to carry out further atrocities;

• the United Kingdom, and United Kingdom nationals are potential targets; and

• Usama Bin Laden and Al Qaida were able to commit these atrocities because of their close alliance with the Taleban régime, which allowed them to operate with impunity in pursuing their terrorist activity.

2. The material in respect of 1998 and the USS *Cole* comes from indictments and intelligence sources. The material in respect of 11 September comes from intelligence and the criminal investigation to date. The details of some aspects cannot be given, but the facts are clear from the intelligence.

3. The document does not contain the totality of the material known to HMG, given the continuing and absolute need to protect intelligence sources.

4. The relevant facts show:

• Al Qaida is a terrorist organisation with ties to a global network, which has been in existence for over 10 years. It was founded, and has been led at all times, by Usama Bin Laden.

• Usama Bin Laden and Al Qaida have been engaged in a jihad against the United States, and its allies. One of their stated aims is the murder of US citizens, and attacks on America's allies.

• Usama Bin Laden and Al Qaida have been based in Afghanistan since 1996, but have a network of operations throughout the world. The network includes training camps, warehouses, communication facilities and commercial operations able to raise significant sums of money to support its activity. That activity includes substantial exploitation of the illegal drugs trade from Afghanistan.

• Usama Bin Laden's Al Qaida and the Taleban régime have a close and mutually dependent alliance. Usama Bin Laden and Al Qaida provide the Taleban régime with material, financial and military support. They jointly exploit the drugs trade. The Taleban régime allows Bin Laden to operate his terrorist training camps and activities from Afghanistan, protects him from attacks from outside, and protects the drugs stockpiles. Usama Bin Laden could not operate his terrorist activities without the alliance and support of the Taleban régime. The Taleban's strength would be seriously weakened without Usama Bin Laden's military and financial support.

• Usama Bin Laden and Al Qaida have the capability to execute major terrorist attacks.

• Usama Bin Laden has claimed credit for the attack on US soldiers in Somalia in October 1993, which killed 18; for the attack on the US Embassies in Kenya and Tanzania in August 1998 which killed 224 and injured nearly 5000; and was linked to the attack on the USS *Cole* on 12 October 2000, in which 17 crew members were killed and 40 others injured.

• They have sought to acquire nuclear and chemical materials for use as terrorist weapons.

In Relation to the Terrorist Attacks on 11 September

• After 11 September we learned that, not long before, Bin Laden had indicated he was about to launch a major attack on America. The detailed planning for the terrorist attacks of 11 September was carried out by one of UBL's close associates. Of the 19 hijackers involved in 11 September 2001, it has been established that the majority had links with Al Qaida. A senior Bin Laden associate claimed to have trained some of the hijackers in Afghanistan. The attacks on 11 September 2001 were similar in both their ambition and intended impact to previous attacks undertaken by Usama Bin Laden and Al Qaida, and also had features in common. In particular:

• Suicide attackers
• Co-ordinated attacks on the same day
• The aim to cause maximum American casualties
• Total disregard for other casualties, including Muslim
• Meticulous long-term planning
• Absence of warning.

6. Al Qaida retains the capability and the will to make further attacks on the US and its allies, including the United Kingdom.

7. Al Qaida gives no warning of terrorist attack.

Usama Bin Laden and Al Qaida

8. In 1989 Usama Bin Laden, and others, founded an international terrorist group known as "Al Qaida" (the Base). At all times he has been the leader of Al Qaida.

9. From 1989 until 1991 Usama Bin Laden was based in Afghanistan and Peshawar, Pakistan. In 1991 he moved to Sudan, where he stayed until 1996. In that year he returned to Afghanistan, where he remains.

The Taleban Régime

10. The Taleban emerged from the Afghan refugee camps in Pakistan in the early 1990s. By 1996 they had captured Kabul. They are still engaged in a bloody civil war to control the whole of Afghanistan. They are led by Mullah Omar.

11. In 1996 Usama Bin Laden moved back to Afghanistan. He established a close relationship with Mullah Omar, and threw his support behind the Taleban. Usama Bin Laden and the Taleban régime have a close alliance on which both depend for their continued existence. They also share the same religious values and vision.

12. Usama Bin Laden has provided the Taleban régime with troops, arms and money to fight the Northern Alliance. He is closely involved with Taleban military training, planning and operations. He has representatives in the Taleban military command structure. He has also given infrastructure assistance and humanitarian aid. Forces under the control of Usama Bin Laden have fought alongside the Taleban in the civil war in Afghanistan.

13. Omar has provided Bin Laden with a safe haven in which to operate, and has allowed him to establish terrorist training camps in Afghanistan. They jointly exploit the Afghan drugs trade. In return for active Al Qaida support, the Taleban allow Al Qaida to operate freely, including planning, training and preparing for terrorist activity. In addition the Taleban provide security for the stockpiles of drugs.

14. Since 1996, when the Taleban captured Kabul, the United States government has consistently raised with them

a whole range of issues, including humanitarian aid and terrorism. Well before 11 September 2001 they had provided evidence to the Taleban of the responsibility of Al Qaida for the terrorist attacks in East Africa. This evidence had been provided to senior leaders of the Taleban at their request.

15. The United States government had made it clear to the Taleban régime that Al Qaida had murdered US citizens, and planned to murder more. The US offered to work with the Taleban to expel the terrorists from Afghanistan. These talks, which have been continuing since 1996, have failed to produce any results.

16. In June 2001, in the face of mounting evidence of the Al Qaida threat, the United States warned the Taleban that it had the right to defend itself and that it would hold the régime responsible for attacks against US citizens by terrorists sheltered in Afghanistan.

17. In this, the United States had the support of the United Nations. The Security Council, in Resolution 1267, condemned Usama Bin Laden for sponsoring international terrorism and operating a network of terrorist camps, and demanded that the Taleban surrender Usama Bin Laden without further delay so that he could be brought to justice.

18. Despite the evidence provided by the US of the responsibility of Usama Bin Laden and Al Qaida for the 1998 East Africa bombings, despite the accurately perceived threats of further atrocities, and despite the demands of the United Nations, the Taleban régime responded by saying no evidence existed against Usama Bin Laden, and that neither he nor his network would be expelled.

19. A former Government official in Afghanistan has described the Taleban and Usama Bin Laden as "two sides of the same coin: Usama cannot exist in Afghanistan without the Taleban and the Taleban cannot exist without Usama".

Al Qaida

20. Al Qaida is dedicated to opposing 'un-Islamic' governments in Muslim countries with force and violence.

21. Al Qaida virulently opposes the United States. Usama

Bin Laden has urged and incited his followers to kill American citizens, in the most unequivocal terms.
22. On 12 October 1996 he issued a declaration of jihad as follows:

> *The people of Islam have suffered from aggression, iniquity and injustice imposed by the Zionist-Crusader alliance and their collaborators . . .*
>
> *It is the duty now on every tribe in the Arabian peninsula to fight jihad and cleanse the land from these Crusader occupiers. Their wealth is booty to those who kill them.*
>
> *My Muslim brothers: your brothers in Palestine and in the land of the two Holy Places* [Saudi Arabia] *are calling upon your help and asking you to take part in fighting against the enemy—the Americans and the Israelis. They are asking you to do whatever you can to expel the enemies out of the sanctities of Islam.*

Later in the same year he said that *"terrorising the American occupiers* [of Islamic Holy Places] *is a religious and logical obligation"*.

In February 1998 he issued and signed a 'fatwa' which included a decree to all Muslims:

> *the killing of Americans and their civilian and military allies is a religious duty for each and every Muslim to be carried out in whichever country they are until Al Aqsa mosque has been liberated from their grasp and until their armies have left Muslim lands.*

In the same 'fatwa' he called on Muslim scholars and their leaders and their youths to *"launch an attack on the American soldiers of Satan"* and concluded:

> *We—with God's help—call on every Muslim who believes in God and wishes to be rewarded to comply with God's order to kill Americans and plunder their money whenever and wherever they find it. We also call on Muslims . . . to launch the raid on Satan's US troops and the devil's supporters allying with them, and to displace those who are behind them.*

When asked, in 1998, about obtaining chemical or nuclear weapons he said *"acquiring such weapons for the defence of Muslims [is] a religious duty"*, and made the following claim in an interview printed in the Pakistan newspaper *Dawn* in November 2001:

> *"I wish to declare that if America used chemical or nuclear weapons against us, then we may retort with chemical and nuclear weapons. We have the weapons as deterrent."*

In an interview aired on Al Jazira (Doha, Qatar) television he stated: *"Our enemy is every American male, whether he is directly fighting us or paying taxes."*

In two interviews broadcast on US television in 1997 and 1998 he referred to the terrorists who carried out the earlier attack on the World Trade Center in 1993 as *"role models"*. He went on to exhort his followers *"to take the fighting to America"*.

23. From the early 1990s Usama Bin Laden has sought to obtain nuclear and chemical materials for use as weapons of terror.

24. Although US targets are Al Qaida's priority, it also explicitly threatens the United States' allies. References to *"Zionist-Crusader alliance and their collaborators"*, and to *"Satan's US troops and the devil's supporters allying with them"* are references which unquestionably include the United Kingdom. This is confirmed by more specific references in a broadcast of 13 October [2001], during which Bin Laden's spokesman said:

> *Al Qaida declares that Bush Sr, Bush Jr, Clinton, Blair and Sharon are the arch-criminals from among the Zionists and Crusaders. . . . Al Qaida stresses that the blood of those killed will not go to waste, God willing, until we punish these criminals. . . . We also say and advise the Muslims in the United States and Britain . . . not to travel by plane. We also advise them not to live in high-rise buildings and towers.*

25. There is a continuing threat. Based on our experience of the way the network has operated in the past, other cells,

like those that carried out the terrorist attacks on 11 September, must be assumed to exist.

26. Al Qaida functions both on its own and through a network of other terrorist organisations. These include Egyptian Islamic Jihad and other north African Islamic extremist terrorist groups, and a number of other jihadi groups in other countries including the Sudan, Yemen, Somalia, Pakistan and India. Al Qaida also maintains cells and personnel in a number of other countries to facilitate its activities.

27. Usama Bin Laden heads the Al Qaida network. Below him is a body known as the Shura, which includes representatives of other terrorist groups, such as Egyptian Islamic Jihad leader Ayman Zawahiri and prominent lieutenants of Bin Laden such as Mohamed Atef (also known as Abu Hafs Al-Masri.) Egyptian Islamic Jihad has, in effect, merged with Al Qaida.

28. In addition to the Shura, Al Qaida has several groups dealing with military, media, financial and Islamic issues.

29. Mohamed Atef is a member of the group that deals with military and terrorist operations. His duties include principal responsibility for training Al Qaida members.

30. Members of Al Qaida must make a pledge of allegiance to follow the orders of Usama Bin Laden.

31. A great deal of evidence about Usama Bin Laden and Al Qaida has been made available in the US indictment for earlier crimes.

32. Since 1989, Usama Bin Laden has conducted substantial financial and business transactions on behalf of Al Qaida and in pursuit of its goals. These include purchasing land for training camps, purchasing warehouses for the storage of items, including explosives, purchasing communications and electronics equipment, and transporting currency and weapons to members of Al Qaida and associated terrorist groups in countries throughout the world.

33. Since 1989 Usama Bin Laden has provided training camps and guest houses in Afghanistan, Pakistan, the Sudan, Somalia and Kenya for the use of Al Qaida and associated terrorist groups. We know from intelligence that there

are currently at least a dozen camps across Afghanistan, of which at least four are used for training terrorists.

34. Since 1989, Usama Bin Laden has established a series of businesses to provide income for Al Qaida, and to provide cover for the procurement of explosives, weapons and chemicals, and for the travel of Al Qaida operatives. The businesses have included a holding company known as 'Wadi Al Aqiq', a construction business known as 'Al Hijra', an agricultural business known as 'Al Themar Al Mubaraka', and investment companies known as 'Ladin International' and 'Taba Investments'.

Usama Bin Laden and Previous Attacks

35. In 1992 and 1993 Mohamed Atef travelled to Somalia on several occasions for the purpose of organising violence against United States and United Nations troops then stationed in Somalia. On each occasion he reported back to Usama Bin Laden, at his base in the Riyadh district of Khartoum.

36. In the spring of 1993 Atef, Saif al Adel, another senior member of Al Qaida, and other members began to provide military training to Somali tribes for the purpose of fighting the United Nations forces.

37. On 3 and 4 October 1993 operatives of Al Qaida participated in the attack on US military personnel serving in Somalia as part of the operation 'Restore Hope.' Eighteen US military personnel were killed in the attack.

38. From 1993 members of Al Qaida began to live in Nairobi and set up businesses there, including Asma Ltd, and Tanzanite King. They were regularly visited there by senior members of Al Qaida, in particular by Atef and Abu Ubadiah al Banshiri.

39. Beginning in the latter part of 1993, members of Al Qaida in Kenya began to discuss the possibility of attacking the US Embassy in Nairobi in retaliation for US participation in Operation Restore Hope in Somalia. Ali Mohamed, a US citizen and admitted member of Al Qaida, surveyed the US Embassy as a possible target for a terrorist attack. He took photographs and made sketches, which he pre-

sented to Usama Bin Laden while Bin Laden was in Sudan. He also admitted that he had trained terrorists for Al Qaida in Afghanistan in the early 1990s, and that those whom he trained included many involved in the East African bombings in August 1998.

40. In June or July 1998, two Al Qaida operatives, Fahid Mohammed Ali Msalam and Sheik Ahmed Salim Swedan, purchased a Toyota truck and made various alterations to the back of the truck.

41. In early August 1998, operatives of Al Qaida gathered in 43, New Runda Estates, Nairobi to execute the bombing of the US Embassy in Nairobi.

42. On 7 August 1998, Assam, a Saudi national and Al Qaida operative, drove the Toyota truck to the US Embassy. There was a large bomb in the back of the truck.

43. Also in the truck was Mohamed Rashed Daoud Al 'Owali, another Saudi. He, by his own confession, was an Al Qaida operative, who from about 1996 had been trained in Al Qaida camps in Afghanistan in explosives, hijacking, kidnapping, assassination and intelligence techniques. With Usama Bin Laden's express permission, he fought alongside the Taleban in Afghanistan. He had met Usama Bin Laden personally in 1996 and asked for another 'mission.' Usama Bin Laden sent him to East Africa after extensive specialised training at camps in Afghanistan.

44. As the truck approached the Embassy, Al 'Owali got out and threw a stun grenade at a security guard. Assam drove the truck up to the rear of the Embassy. He got out and then detonated the bomb, which demolished a multi-storey secretarial college and severely damaged the US Embassy, and the Co-operative bank building. The bomb killed 213 people and injured 4500. Assam was killed in the explosion.

45. Al 'Owali expected the mission to end in his death. He had been willing to die for Al Qaida. But at the last minute he ran away from the bomb truck and survived. He had no money, passport or plan to escape after the mission, because he had expected to die.

46. After a few days, he called a telephone number in

Yemen to have money transferred to him in Kenya. The number he rang in Yemen was contacted by Usama Bin Laden's phone on the same day as Al 'Owali was arranging to get the money.

47. Another person arrested in connection with the Nairobi bombing was Mohamed Sadeek Odeh. He admitted to his involvement. He identified the principal participants in the bombing. He named three other persons, all of whom were Al Qaida or Egyptian Islamic Jihad members.

48. In Dar es Salaam the same day, at about the same time, operatives of Al Qaida detonated a bomb at the US Embassy, killing 11 people. The Al Qaida operatives involved included Mustafa Mohamed Fadhil and Khaflan Khamis Mohamed. The bomb was carried in a Nissan Atlas truck, which Ahmed Khfaklan Ghailani and Sheikh Ahmed Salim Swedan, two Al Qaida operatives, had purchased in July 1998, in Dar es Salaam.

49. Khaflan Khamis Mohamed was arrested for the bombing. He admitted membership of Al Qaida, and implicated other members of Al Qaida in the bombing.

50. On 7 and 8 August 1998, two other members of Al Qaida disseminated claims of responsibility for the two bombings by sending faxes to media organisations in Paris, Doha in Qatar, and Dubai in the United Arab Emirates.

51. Additional evidence of the involvement of Al Qaida in the East African bombings came from a search conducted in London of several residences and businesses belonging to Al Qaida and Egyptian Islamic Jihad members. In those searches a number of documents were found including claims of responsibility for the East African bombings in the name of a fictitious group, 'the Islamic Army for the liberation of the Holy Places'.

52. Al 'Owali, the would-be suicide bomber, admitted he was told to make a videotape of himself using the name of the same fictitious group.

53. The faxed claims of responsibility were traced to a telephone number, which had been in contact with Usama Bin Laden's cell phone. The claims disseminated to the

press were clearly written by someone familiar with the conspiracy. They stated that the bombings had been carried out by two Saudis in Kenya, and one Egyptian in Dar es Salaam. They were probably sent before the bombings had even taken place. They referred to two Saudis dying in the Nairobi attack. In fact, because Al 'Owali fled at the last minute, only one Saudi died.

54. On 22 December 1998 Usama Bin Laden was asked by *Time* magazine whether he was responsible for the August 1998 attacks. He replied:

The International Islamic Jihad Front for the jihad against the US and Israel has, by the grace of God, issued a crystal clear fatwa calling on the Islamic nation to carry on Jihad aimed at liberating the holy sites. The nation of Mohammed has responded to this appeal. If instigation for jihad against the Jews and the Americans . . . is considered to be a crime, then let history be a witness that I am a criminal. Our job is to instigate and, by the grace of God, we did that, and certain people responded to this instigation.

He was asked if he knew the attackers: *"Those who risked their lives to earn the pleasure of God are real men. They managed to rid the Islamic nation of disgrace. We hold them in the highest esteem."*

And what the US could expect of him:

any thief or criminal who enters another country to steal should expect to be exposed to murder at any time. . . . The US knows that I have attacked it, by the grace of God, for more than ten years now. . . . God knows that we have been pleased by the killing of American soldiers [in Somalia in 1993]. This was achieved by the grace of God and the efforts of the mujahideen. . . . Hostility towards America is a religious duty and we hope to be rewarded for it by God. I am confident that Muslims will be able to end the legend of the so-called superpower that is America.

55. In December 1999 a terrorist cell linked to Al Qaida was discovered trying to carry out attacks inside the United States. An Algerian, Ahmed Ressam, was stopped at the US-Canadian border, and over 100 lbs of bomb-making material

was found in his car. Ressam admitted he was planning to set off a large bomb at Los Angeles International airport on New Year's Day. He said that he had received terrorist training at Al Qaida camps in Afghanistan and then been instructed to go abroad and kill US civilians and military personnel.

56. On 3 January 2000, a group of Al Qaida members, and other terrorists who had trained in Al Qaida camps in Afghanistan, attempted to attack a US destroyer with a small boat loaded with explosives. Their boat sank, aborting the attack.

57. On 12 October 2000, however, the USS *Cole* was struck by an explosive-laden boat while refuelling in Aden harbour. Seventeen crew were killed, and 40 injured.

58. Several of the perpetrators of the *Cole* attack (mostly Yemenis and Saudis) were trained at Usama Bin Laden's camps in Afghanistan. Al 'Owali has indentified the two commanders of the attack on the USS *Cole* as having participated in the planning and preparation for the East African Embassy bombings.

59. In the months before the 11 September attacks, propaganda videos were distributed throughout the Middle East and Muslim world by Al Qaida, in which Usama Bin Laden and others were shown encouraging Muslims to attack American and Jewish targets.

60. Similar videos, extolling violence against the United States and other targets, were distributed before the East African Embassy attacks in August 1998.

Usama Bin Laden and the 11 September Attacks

61. Nineteen men have been identified as the hijackers from the passenger lists of the four planes hijacked on 11 September 2001. Many of them had previous links with Al Qaida or have so far been positively identified as associates of Al Qaida. An associate of some of the hijackers has been identified as playing key roles in both the East African Embassy attacks and the USS *Cole* attack. Investigations continue into the backgrounds of all the hijackers.

62. From intelligence sources, the following facts have been established subsequent to 11 September; for intelligence reasons, the names of associates, though known, are not given.

- In the run-up to 11 September, Bin Laden was mounting a concerted propaganda campaign amongst likeminded groups of people—including videos and documentation—justifying attacks on Jewish and American targets; and claiming that those who died in the course of them were carrying out God's work.
- We have learned, subsequent to 11 September, that Bin Laden himself asserted shortly before 11 September that he was preparing a major attack on America.
- In August and early September close associates of Bin Laden were warned to return to Afghanistan from other parts of the world by 10 September.
- Immediately prior to 11 September some known associates of Bin Laden were naming the date for action as on or around 11 September.
- A senior associate claimed to have trained some of the hijackers in Afghanistan.
- Since 11 September we have learned that one of Bin Laden's closest and most senior associates was responsible for the detailed planning of the attacks.
- There is evidence of a very specific nature relating to the guilt of Bin Laden and his associates that is too sensitive to release.

63. In addition, Usama Bin Laden has issued a number of public statements since the US strikes on Afghanistan began. The language used in these, while not an open admission of guilt, is self-incriminating.

64. For example, on 7 October he said:

Here is America struck by God Almighty in one of its vital organs, so that its greatest buildings are destroyed. Grace and gratitude to God . . . I swear to God that America will not live in peace before peace reigns in Palestine, and before all the army of infidels depart the land of Mohammed, peace be upon him.

65. On 9 October his spokesman praised the *"good deed"*

of the hijackers, who *"transferred the battle into the US heartland"*. He warned that the *"storm of plane attacks will not abate"*.

66. On 20 October Bin Laden gave an inflammatory interview which has been circulating, in the form of a video, among supporters in the Al Qaida network. In the transcript, when referring to the US buildings that were attacked, he says:

> *It is what we instigated for a while, in self-defence. And it was in revenge for our people killed in Palestine and Iraq. So if avenging the killing of our people is terrorism, let history be a witness that we are terrorists.*

Later in the interview he said:

> *Bush and Blair . . . don't understand any language but the language of force. Every time they kill us, we will kill them, so the balance of terror can be achieved.*

He went on:

> *The battle has been moved inside America, and we shall continue until we win this battle, or die in the cause and meet our maker.*

He also said:

> *The bad terror is what America and Israel are practising against our people, and what we are practising is the good terror that will stop them doing what they are doing.*

67. Usama Bin Laden remains in charge, and the mastermind, of Al Qaida. In Al Qaida, an operation on the scale of the 11 September attacks would have been approved by Usama Bin Laden himself.

68. The modus operandi of 11 September was entirely consistent with previous attacks. Al Qaida's record of atrocities is characterised by meticulous long-term planning, a desire to inflict mass casualties, suicide bombers, and multiple simultaneous attacks.

69. The attacks of 11 September 2001 are entirely con-

sistent with the scale and sophistication of the planning which went into the attacks on the East African Embassies and the USS *Cole*. No warnings were given for these three attacks, just as there was none on 11 September.

70. Al Qaida operatives, in evidence given in the East African Embassy bomb trials, have described how the group spends years preparing for an attack. They conduct repeated surveillance, patiently gather materials, and identify and vet operatives, who have the skills to participate in the attack and the willingness to die for their cause.

71. The operatives involved in the 11 September atrocities attended flight schools, used flight simulators to study the controls of larger aircraft and placed potential airports and routes under surveillance.

72. Al Qaida's attacks are characterised by total disregard for innocent lives, including Muslims. In an interview after the East African bombings, Usama Bin Laden insisted that the need to attack the United States excused the killing of other innocent civilians, Muslim and non-Muslim alike.

73. No other organisation has both the motivation and the capability to carry out attacks like those of the 11 September—only the Al Qaida network under Usama Bin Laden.

Conclusion

74. The attacks of the 11 September 2001 were planned and carried out by Al Qaida, an organisation whose head is Usama Bin Laden. That organisation has the will, and the resources, to execute further attacks of similar scale. Both the United States and its close allies are targets for such attacks. The attack could not have occurred without the alliance between the Taleban and Usama Bin Laden, which allowed Bin Laden to operate freely in Afghanistan, promoting, planning and executing terrorist activity.

Excerpted from *Responsibility for the Terrorist Atrocities in the United States, 11 September 2001—An Updated Account,* by Tony Blair, November 14, 2001.

Chronology

September 11, 2001

7:59 A.M. EDT

American Airlines Flight 11 leaves Boston's Logan Airport, bound for Los Angeles, carrying ninety-two passengers and crew.

8:01 A.M.

United Airlines Flight 93 leaves Newark, New Jersey, for San Francisco with forty-five people aboard.

8:10 A.M.

American Airlines Flight 77 departs Washington, D.C.'s Dulles Airport for Los Angeles with sixty-four people on board.

8:14 A.M.

United Airlines Flight 175 takes off from Boston's Logan Airport for Los Angeles with sixty-five passengers and crew.

8:28 A.M.

American Flight 11 veers off course, south toward New York. An air traffic controller overhears conversation from the cockpit and realizes the plane has been hijacked.

8:46 A.M.

American Flight 11 crashes into the north tower, Tower One, of the World Trade Center between the ninety-fourth and ninety-eighth floors. (Some accounts give the time as 8:48 A.M.)

9:03 A.M.
United Flight 175 crashes into the south tower, Tower Two, of the World Trade Center between the seventy-eighth and eighty-fourth floors.

9:05 A.M.
President George W. Bush, visiting an elementary school in Sarasota, Florida, is notified that two planes have crashed into the World Trade Center.

9:31 A.M.
Bush gives a short speech on television and calls the crashes "an apparent terrorist attack on our country."

9:43 A.M.
American Flight 77 crashes into the Pentagon. Wall Street shuts down. A television station in Abu Dhabi reports that it received a call from the Democratic Front for the Liberation of Palestine claiming responsibility for the attacks; the claim is later denied. The U.S. Capitol and the White House are evacuated.

9:49 A.M.
The Federal Aviation Administration grounds all flights in the United States. Planes are directed to land at the nearest airport; international flights are either diverted to Canada or turned back.

9:58 A.M.
An emergency operator in Pennsylvania receives a phone call from a passenger on board United Flight 93 who says the plane has been hijacked.

9:59 A.M.
Tower Two, the second tower to be attacked, collapses.

10:00–11:30 A.M.

All U.S. government buildings across the country are evacuated; the United Nations closes down; New York City mayor Rudy Giuliani orders that Lower Manhattan be evacuated.

10:06 A.M.

United Flight 93 crashes in a field near Shanksville, Pennsylvania, about eighty miles southeast of Pittsburgh.

10:25 A.M.

News anchors report that a car bomb exploded outside the State Department in Washington, D.C. The report is later found to be untrue.

10:29 A.M.

World Trade Center Tower One collapses.

10:50 A.M.

The damaged portion of the Pentagon collapses.

1:04 P.M.

Bush tells the nation that U.S. military forces are on their highest alert, and the United States will "hunt down and punish" whoever is responsible for the attacks.

1:27 P.M.

Anthony A. Williams, the mayor of Washington, D.C., declares a state of emergency.

2:48 P.M.

Giuliani says the death toll from the attacks and collapse is "more than any of us can bear."

4:25 P.M.

The New York Stock Exchange, the American Stock Exchange, and NASDAQ all announce that they will remain closed the following day.

5:20 P.M.
World Trade Center Seven, a forty-seven-story building, collapses.

5:30 P.M.
Government officials claim that United Flight 93 was headed toward Washington, D.C., possibly for the White House or U.S. Capitol, before it crashed in Pennsylvania.

6:54 P.M.
Bush arrives in Washington, D.C., on Air Force One, after making stops at Barksdale Air Force Base in Louisiana and Offut Air Force Base in Nebraska.

7:30 P.M.
Congress announces its bipartisan support for Bush in searching for and punishing whoever is responsible for the attacks. Members sing "God Bless America" on the steps of the U.S. Capitol.

8:30 P.M.
Bush addresses the nation in a nationally televised speech and says that the United States will go after the "terrorists who committed these acts and those who harbor them."

September 12, 2001

Members of the North Atlantic Treaty Organization invoke Article Five of the Washington Treaty for the first time in NATO's history. Article Five states that an attack against one member is an attack against them all; Bush visits the Pentagon; law enforcement officials announce that a car they believe belonged to the hijackers was confiscated at a parking garage at Logan Airport in Boston. Hotels used by the hijackers are also raided; the *Jerusalem Post* reports that Osama bin Laden denies responsibility for the attacks.

September 13, 2001

Queen Elizabeth orders that "The Star-Spangled Banner" be played during the changing of the guard at Buckingham Palace in London; Secretary of State Colin Powell names Osama bin Laden as the prime suspect behind the attacks; U.S. officials release the names of nineteen men who they believe are responsible for hijacking the four planes; the "black box"—the flight data recorder from United Flight 93—is recovered from the crash site in Pennsylvania.

September 14, 2001

The cockpit voice recorder and the flight data recorder are recovered from American Flight 77 at the Pentagon; Europe observes three minutes of silence in memory of the victims of the attacks; September 14 was declared a National Day of Prayer and Remembrance by Bush, who attends a service at the National Cathedral in Washington, D.C.; Bush declares a state of emergency and calls up 500,000 reservists; Bush visits Ground Zero in New York City; the cockpit recorder for United Flight 93 is recovered in Pennsylvania; the Department of Defense announces that 125 Pentagon workers are missing.

September 15, 2001

All commercial airports reopen except for Reagan National Airport in Washington, D.C.; Bush names bin Laden as the lead suspect in organizing the attacks; Pakistan agrees to allow U.S. military forces to use Pakistani bases for staging areas and to fly over its airspace.

September 19, 2001

More than one hundred military aircraft—including fighters, bombers, and support planes—are ordered to the Persian Gulf. Three carrier groups will also soon be in the area.

September 30, 2001

The Taliban—the fundamentalist Islamic government in Afghanistan—admits to the Pakistani ambassador that it is hiding bin Laden somewhere in the country.

October 4, 2001

Limited service begins at Reagan National Airport for the first time since it was shut down on September 11; Great Britain's Prime Minister Tony Blair presents evidence to Parliament showing that bin Laden was involved with the attacks against the United States.

October 7, 2001

A U.S.-led coalition begins a bombing campaign in Afghanistan. Targeted are Taliban military bases and communication facilities and suspected terrorist training camps; bin Laden releases a videotaped statement recorded before the attacks began.

For Further Research

Yonah Alexander and Michael S. Swetnam, *Osama bin Laden's al-Qaida: Profile of a Terrorist Network*. Ardsley, NY: Transnational Publishers, 2001.

Peter L. Bannon, ed., *America's Heroes: Inspiring Stories of Courage, Sacrifice, and Patriotism*. Champaign, IL: SP, LLC, 2001.

Jenny Baxter and Malcolm Downing, eds., *The BBC Reports: On America, Its Allies and Enemies, and the Counterattack on Terrorism*. Woodstock, NY: Overlook Press, 2002.

Beliefnet, ed., *From the Ashes: A Spiritual Response to the Attack on America*. Emmaus, PA: Rodale, 2001.

Thomas Beller, ed., *Before and After: Stories from New York*. New York: Mr. Beller's Neighborhood Books, 2002.

BlueEar.com, ed., *09/11 8:48 A.M.: Documenting America's Greatest Tragedy*. Charleston, SC: BookSurge.com, 2001.

David Bresnahan, *9-11: Terror in America*. Waxahachie, TX: Windsor House, 2001.

Roger Burbach and Ben Clarke, eds., *September 11 and the U.S. War: Beyond the Curtain of Smoke*. San Francisco: City Lights Books, 2002.

Jack Canfield, Mark Victor Hansen, and Matthew E. Adams, eds., *Chicken Soup for the Soul of America: Stories to Heal the Heart of Our Nation*. Deerfield Beach, FL: Health Communications, Inc., 2002.

Noam Chomsky, *9-11*. New York: Seven Stories Press, 2001.

Stephanie J. Clement, ed., *Civilization Under Attack: September 11, 2001, and Beyond: An Astrological Perspective*. St. Paul, MN: Llewellyn, 2001.

Jim Cymbala with Stephen Sorenson, *God's Grace from Ground Zero: Seeking God's Heart for the Future of Our World*. Grand Rapids, MI: Zondervan, 2001.

Der Spiegel Magazine, ed., *Inside 9-11: What Really Happened*. New York: St. Martin's Press, 2001.

Fire Engineering, *Fallen Heroes: A Tribute from Fire Engineering, September 11, 2001*. Tulsa, OK: Pennwell, 2001.

Allison Gilbert et al., eds., *Covering Catastrophe: Broadcast Journalists Report September 11*. Chicago: Bonus Books, 2002.

John Hagee, *Attack on America: New York, Jerusalem, and the Role of Terrorism in the Last Days*. Nashville: T. Nelson, 2001.

David Halberstam, *Firehouse*. New York: Hyperion, 2002.

Fred Halliday, *Two Hours That Shook the World: September 11, 2001: Causes and Consequences*. London: Saqi Books, 2002.

Victor David Hanson, *An Autumn of War: What America Learned from September 11 and the War on Terrorism*. New York: Anchor Books, 2002.

Tony Hendra, *Brotherhood*. New York: American Express, 2001.

James F. Hoge Jr. and Gideon Rose, eds., *How Did This Happen? Terrorism and the New War*. New York: PublicAffairs, 2001.

Grant R. Jeffrey, *War on Terror: Unfolding Bible Prophecy*. Toronto: Frontier Research Publications, 2002.

Bernard B. Kerik, *The Lost Son: A Life in Pursuit of Justice*. New York: Regan Books, 2001.

Life, ed., *One Nation: America Remembers September 11, 2001*. Boston: Little, Brown, 2001.

Magnum Photographers, eds., *New York: September 11*. New York: Powerhouse Books, 2001.

Greg Manning, *Love, Greg and Lauren.* New York: Bantam, 2002.

Mark Miller and Jason File, *Terrorism Factbook: Our Nation at War!* Peoria, IL: Bollix Books, 2001.

James W. Moore, *9/11: What a Difference a Day Makes.* Nashville: Dimensions for Living, 2002.

John Francis Murphy, *Sword of Islam: Muslim Extremism from the Arab Conquests to the Attack on America.* Amherst, NY: Prometheus, 2002.

Michael Parenti, *The Terrorism Trap: September 11 and Beyond.* San Francisco: City Lights Books, 2002.

Richard Picciotto with Daniel Paisner, *Last Man Down: A New York City Fire Chief and the Collapse of the World Trade Center.* New York: Berkley Books, 2002.

Poynter Institute, ed., *September 11, 2001: A Collection of Newspaper Front Pages Selected by the Poynter Institute.* Kansas City, MO: Andrews McMeel, 2001.

Martha Simmons and Frank A. Thomas, eds., *9.11.01: African American Leaders Respond to an American Tragedy.* Valley Forge, PA: Judson Press, 2001.

Dennis Smith, ed., *Report from Ground Zero: The Story of the Rescue Efforts at the World Trade Center.* New York: Viking, 2002.

Strobe Talbott and Nayan Chanda, eds., *The Age of Terror: America and the World After September 11.* New York: Basic Books, 2001.

Katrina vanden Heuvel, *A Just Response: The Nation on Terrorism, Democracy, and September 11, 2001.* New York: Thunder's Mouth Press, 2002.

Jackie Waldman with Brenda Welchlin and Karen Frost, eds., *America September 11: The Courage to Give.* Berkeley, CA: Conari Press, 2001.

Rowan Williams, *Writing in the Dust: After September 11.* Grand Rapids, MI: William B. Eerdmans, 2002.

Index

Abbas, Muhammad, 152
Abdel-Rahman, Omar, 14
Afghanistan
  Arab retaliation for bombing
    of, 155–56
  bombing of, 27–28
  see also Taliban
Africa, 15–16
airplanes
  flight lessons, 24–25
  flights, 20
Alhazmi, Nawaf, 25
Almihdar, Khalid, 25
Alomari, Abdulaziz, 17
Alshehri, Waleed, 24
American Airlines Flight 11,
  17, 31
American Airlines Flight 77,
  17, 19–20
Americans. See civilians;
  survivors
American Society of Engineers,
  70, 71
Apostol, Faustino, 82, 90
Arab Americans, 143–45
  see also September 11
    terrorist attack, Arab
    response to
Atef, Muhammad, 16
Atta, Mohamed, 17, 25

Beamer, Todd, 21
Bertocci, Erin, 110
Bingham, Mark, 21
bin Laden, Osama, 149, 157
  on America's Ten Most

Wanted list, 16
  blamed for September 11
    attack, 26
  dreams and visions of, 163
  gaining followers, 160–61
  holy war declared by, 15, 168,
    169
  organization formed by, 13
  on U.S. troops in Saudi
    Arabia, 14
Blaich, Billy, 86–87
Blair, Tony, 121
  on fighting terrorism, 124–26
  on September 11 attack,
    121–24
  support of United States by,
    23, 117
Boyle, Jimmy, 95
Brooklyn Heights, New York,
  137–38
Brown, Paddy, 79, 90, 95
Buckingham Palace, 116
Burke, Billy, 81
Burnett, Deena, 21
Burnett, Tom, 21
Bush, George W., 118
  on bin Laden, 26
  declaring war on terrorism, 23
  reassurance by, 116–17
  on the Taliban, 26–27
  warned about terrorist attacks,
    26
Butler, Billy, 53, 82, 88

Campanelli, Michele Wallace,
  133

Carter, Mike, 95
casualties. *See* September 11
  terrorist attack, casualties
Chelsea Piers, 104–105
Childs, Craig, 112
civilians
  anger and sadness by, 116
  bringing food and supplies to
    rescue workers, 110–14
  helping each other outside of
    World Trade Center, 35, 69
  neighborly concern among,
    137–41
  racism toward Arab
    Americans by, 143–45
  searching for American flag,
    133–36
  in the streets, following the
    attack, 62–65, 108
  see also survivors; victims
Clark, Brian, 38
Coll, Bobby, 42, 43, 45
Coulter, Ann, 135

Dabner, Chris, 86
DeDominico, Jim, 89–90
DiFrancesco, Ron, 43–45
dogs
  police, 51, 54, 55
  search and rescue, 100,
    101–103
Downey, Ray, 95

Embry-Riddle Aeronautical
  University, 25
Empire State Building, 20
England, 116, 122
evacuation
  of New York City public
    buildings, 20
  of White House and U.S.
    Capitol, 20

of World Trade Center, 32
  evacuees helping each other
    during, 44–45, 49–50
  evacuee's personal account
    of, 34–35
  knowledge of collapse and,
    75–76
  meeting firefighters on the
    stairs during, 31, 35, 80–81
  orders to return to offices
    and, 40–41
  survivor's personal account
    of, 43–44, 45–48

Falco, Tommy, 53, 82
fatwas, 14, 15, 169
FBI (Federal Bureau of
  Investigation), 24, 26
Federal Aviation Administration
  (FAA), 20
Feehan, Bill, 93
fire
  as different from other World
    Trade Center fires, 75
  observed from Manhattan
    Bridge, 78
firefighters
  casualties among, 76
  climbing up World Trade
    Center stairs, 31, 35, 80–81
  driving to World Trade Center,
    78–79, 92–93
  evacuating building after
    collapse, 81–83, 84–85
  finding human remains,
    101–102
  inspiration from, 95–96
  learning of collapse of Tower
    One, 81
  lost and missing, 94–95
  personal account of airplane
    crash by, 79–80

rescuing each other, 85–87,
    88–90
returning to firehouse, 90–91
in survival mode while
    trapped in stairwell, 87–88
waiting to get orders, 79
see also rescue efforts/workers
flag (American)
displaying, 134, 136
flown half-mast by German
    ship, 132
meaning of, 136
searching for, 133, 134–35
flight lessons, 24–25
Forgey, Benjamin, 70, 71
Fredericks, Andy, 81

Gallagher, Kevin, 95, 96
Ganci, Peter, 93
Garcia, Louis, 18–19
Gellman, Barton, 21–22
German navy, 132
Ghaith, Sulaiman Abu, 154
Giuliani, Rudy
on New York City, 127–28
reassurance by, 116–17
on St. Paul's Chapel, 129
on victims, 128
Glick, Jeremy, 21
Ground Zero
bringing food and supplies to
    rescue workers at, 110–11,
    113–14
described by civilian, 111–13
makeshift morgues in, 97–99
priest at, 105–10
searching for bodies at,
    100–103
see also World Trade Center
Grove, Elizabeth, 137

Hallinan, Megan, 131

Hanjour, Hani, 25
Haring, Tom, 86
Harris, Josephine, 82–85
Hatton, Terry, 79–80, 90, 95
Hayden, Pete, 79, 89–90
Hickey, Brian, 95
Hitch, Munter, 88

Iraq, 168, 169
Islam
as alive and well, 153
does not endorse violence,
    148, 166–70
nations of, as suffering,
    154–55
"true," 160
victory for, 162
Islamic fundamentalism, 124
Israel. *See* State of Israel
Israeli-Palestinian conflict, 147

Jauher, Sandeep, 97
jihad, 155, 169
Jonas, Jay, 77

Komoroski, Matt, 85, 87
Kross, Mickey, 85
Kuwait, 13

Labriola, John, 33
Levey, Bob, 142
Lim, Dave, 51
al-Luheidan, Salih bin
    Muhammad, 166

Manning, Greg, 67
Manning, Lauren, 67–73
Marrero, Jose, 46
Martin, James, 104
McKenna, Terrence, 16
Meldrum, Mike, 53, 88–89
Metropolitan Museum of Art, 20

Middle East crisis, 147
Mogadishu, Somalia, 14
Morgan, Paul, 100
morgue, makeshift, 97–99,
   106–107
Moussaoui, Zacarias, 25
mullahs, 148
Muslims
   on U.S. troops in Saudi
      Arabia, 14
   see also Islam; September 11
      terrorist attack, Arab
      response to

Nacke, Lou, 21
NATO (North Atlantic Treaty
   Organization), 23–24
Nevins, Jerry, 79–80, 90
New York City
   Giuliani on, 127–28
   neighborly concern in, 137–41
Nigeria, 15–16
9/11 terrorist attack. *See*
   September 11 terrorist attack

O'Clery, Conor, 56
Office of Homeland Security, 27
al-Owhali, Mohamed Rashed
   Daoud, 16

Palestinian-Israel conflict, 147
patriotism, 133–36
Pauline, Jim, 135
Pearl Harbor, 142–43
Pentagon attack, 19–20, 22
Persian Gulf War (1990–1991),
   13
Pfeifer, Joe, 79
physicians, 97–99
Picciotto, Rich, 82, 88
police dogs, 51, 54, 55
police officers

casualties among, 76
explosive detection by, 51
helping priest to subway, 109
priest talking to, 107–108
rescue efforts by, 54
trapped in World Trade
   Center, 52–54
see also rescue efforts/workers
Port Authority of New York,
   51–55, 76
Praimnath, Stanley, 44–50
priests, 104–109
Prunty, Richard, 85, 90

al-Qaeda
   terrorist attacks by, 14, 16,
      168
   see also bin Laden, Osama

rescue efforts/workers, 18–19
   bringing food and supplies to,
      110–14
   calling 911, 47–48
   by evacuee in World Trade
      Center, 44–45
   inspiration from, 107, 113–14
   in Pentagon building, 20
   Rudy Giuliani on, 128–29
   searching for bodies, 100–103
   see also firefighters; police
      officers
Ridge, Tom, 27
Rohan, Glenn, 89

Salka, John, 86
Saudi Arabia
   Persian Gulf War and, 13–14
   post–September 11 sermons
      in, 158–59
   terrorist attack in, 14
search and rescue dogs, 100,
   101–103

search and rescue efforts,
100–103
September 11 terrorist attack
Arab response to, 147–48
on acceptance of Islam, 160
disagreeing with killing of
innocent people, 166–70
on dreams and visions of
terrorist attack, 163, 164,
165
on duty of jihad, 155–56
on Islamic victory, 162
joy and happiness, 161–62
lack of tears for America,
152–53
by Osama bin Laden, 150–51
in sermons in Saudi Arabia,
158–59
on suffering of Islamic
nation, 154–55
thanks and praise to bin
Laden, 158
casualties, 23, 76
British citizens, 122–23
compared with other
British tragedies, 123
Pentagon attack, 20
United Airlines Flight 93, 21
missed clues by American
government on, 25–26
motivations for, 13–14
planning for, 16–17
sequence of attacks, 17–23
St. Paul's Chapel surviving,
129
Western response to
by Buckingham Palace, 116
by Bush, 23, 116–17,
118–20
by NATO, 23–24
by overseas military officers,
131

by Rudy Giuliani, 116–17,
127–30
support by German navy,
132
by Tony Blair, 117, 121–24
by United Nations, 24
see also civilians
see also terrorists; victims;
World Trade Center
al-Shehhi, Marwan, 25
Smith, Dennis, 92
Somalia, 14
Somerset County,
Pennsylvania, 21
"Star Spangled Banner," 134
State of Israel, 147
St. Paul's Chapel, 129
survivors
on collapse of World Trade
Center, 36
on crash into World Trade
Center, 33–34, 39–40, 42–43
emotional response by, 66
on evacuation from World
Trade Center, 34–35, 40–41,
43–44, 45–48
expectations for more, 105
helping each other, 44–45,
49–50
on outside of World Trade
Center, 35–36
returning home, 36–37, 65
trying to call 911, 47–48
watching a friend die, 65–66
see also civilians

Taliban
Bush on, 26–27
U.S. demands of, 27
Tanzania, 15–16
terrorism
by America, 155

attempted at Los Angeles International Airport, 16
bombing of military barracks in Saudi Arabia, 14
embassy bombings in Africa (1998), 15–16
murder of Americans in Somalia (1993), 14
1993 World Trade Center bombing, 14
by al-Qaeda, 168
Tony Blair on fighting, 124–26
USS *Cole* bombing, 16
will continue in America, 153, 155–56
terrorists
flight lessons by, 24–25
identifying, 24
knowledge of operation by, 164
Townsend, Timothy, 61

United Airlines Flight 93, 17, 20–21
United Airlines Flight 175, 17–18, 31
United Nations, 20, 24
Security Council, 124
United States, the
bin Laden's holy war against, 168, 169
Capitol building, 20
defending freedom in, 130
demands to Taliban by, 27
hypocrisy by, 150–51
new cabinet level position in, 27
strength and resilience of, 118–19
united in wanting peace and security, 119–20

as vulnerable to pain and death, 152–53
see also Bush, George W.; September 11 terrorist attack, Western response to

Vera, David, 43–46
victims
burn, 67–73
makeshift morgues for, 97–99, 106–107
Rudy Giuliani on, 128
searching for, 100–103
Visconti, Sal, 86

Warchola, Mike, 82, 85, 90
Weiss, Dave, 79–80, 90
White House, 20
Wilson, Hal, 100, 103
World Trade Center, the
collapse of, 21–22
engineers' report on reasons for, 70, 71
eyewitness account of, 58–59
firefighter's personal account of, 81, 83–84
police officer's personal account of, 52–54
survivor's personal account of, 36
crashing of airplanes into, 31
eyewitness account of, 56–57
first plane, 17, 18
floor location, 75
heard by firefighter, 78, 79–80
police officer's account of, 52
survivor's personal account of, 33–34, 39–40
deaths at, 76

evacuation of, 32
  evacuees helping each other
    during, 44–45, 49–50
  evacuee's personal account
    of, 34–35
  knowledge of collapse and,
    75–76
  meeting firefighters on the
    stairs during, 31, 35, 80–81
  orders to return to offices
    and, 40–41
  survivor's personal account
    of, 43–44, 45–48

fire in, 75
1993 bombing of, 14
outside, following terrorist
  attack, 35, 36–37, 49, 60, 62,
  93–94
people jumping from, 32, 57,
  62, 63
see also evacuation; Ground
  Zero

York, Kevin, 43, 45
Yousef, Ramzi, 14